A DOZEN ORGIES

"Sound, intelligent, exciting contemporary theatre… This is a fine collection of plays that not only represents good Latin American authors but also sound and effective theatre… The plays are all 'engaging' in one way or another. They should have production appeal… As a director I could make any of them work… and work well."

William I. Oliver, Stage Director and Professor of Theatre Arts, University of California, Berkeley

"Excellent… Intelligently and imaginatively selected and well translated. I enjoyed reading [the collection.] There is a good combination of well-established and not-so-well-known authors, which seems an advantage in this kind of anthology."

Margaret S. Peden, Professor of Latin American Drama, University of Missouri at Columbia

A DOZEN ORGIES

Latin American Plays Of the 20th Century

Edited and Translated

By

ROBERT S. RUDDER

SVENSON Publishers
2013

All Rights Reserved. Translation and publication of all dramas in this anthology have been expressly authorized by their individual authors. Inquiries for permission to perform these plays, or any other questions concerning these plays should be addressed to SVENSON Publishers, 1556 Lafayette Rd., Claremont, CA. 91711, or Rddrbor@aol.com.

Copyright © 2013 by SVENSON Publishers
Claremont, CA.

ISBN-13:978-0615842776
ISBN-10:0615842771

Cover illustration by José Guadalupe Posada

Several of the translations in this anthology were first printed as rough drafts in *Drama and Theatre*, 1972, and in the anthology, *The Orgy*, issued by the Latin American Center of the University of California, Los Angeles (©1974 The Regents of the University of California). I would like to express my appreciation to the Latin American Center and Gerardo Luzuriaga, who originally compared my work to the Spanish versions, for giving me permission to publish these translations, now in their corrected and revised form.

Robert S. Rudder

A DOZEN ORGIES

Contents

PREFATORY NOTE 7
THE ORGY 9
THE SCHOOLTEACHER 27
THE STORY OF THE MAN WHO TURNED INTO A DOG 33
THE STORY OF PANCHITO GONZÁLEZ 43
R.I.P. 53
ROMEO BEFORE THE CORPSE OF JULIET 67
YOU DON'T HAVE TO COMPLICATE HAPPINESS ... 73
BLACK LIGHT 77
MARCH 115
THE DEATH OF ALFRED GREY 125
THE CRUCIFIXION 155
THE EVE OF THE EXECUTION 169

ROBERT S. RUDDER

PREFATORY NOTE

From colonial times through the nineteenth century, theatre in Latin America was primarily influenced by that of Europe: Spanish Golden Age comedies, neoclassical pieces, then romanticism. Traveling companies from Spain first brought their works to the New World, then individual regions began to produce their own brand of theatre, often with local music and dance playing an important part. Permanent theatres received support from the government beginning in the eighteenth century, while in the twentieth century vanguard movements also sprang up, mainly in the universities, exploring first the realism of Henrik Ibsen, and then the experimental theatre of German Expressionism and the Theatre of the Absurd (Brecht, Beckett, Ionesco, Pirandello, etc.). It is this period of experimentation that we see largely embodied in the plays of this collection. These dramatists often show us a world in which human existence seems to have no meaning or purpose, and where man is threatened or controlled by incomprehensible and illogical forces. At the same time, these Latin American playwrights offer a stinging critique of the social and political forces at work in their individual countries. If we look more closely, however, we discover that their message is not merely local: it applies to the world at large.

The translations in this collection, representing some of the best dramatists of Latin America, have been presented on stage numerous times throughout the United States, Canada, and Europe, and have been broadcast by the BBC.

THE ORGY

ENRIQUE BUENAVENTURA

ENRIQUE BUENAVENTURA

ENRIQUE BUENAVENTURA

Colombia: 1924-2003.

Living a Bohemian life-style, Buenaventura was a sailor, an actor, a self-taught painter and sculptor, and a writer of poetry, stories, essays and award-winning dramas. He traveled though several Latin American countries before returning to his birthplace of Cali, Colombia, where he worked for both regional and national theatre groups. In 1955 he co-founded the Teatro Experimental de Cali (TEC) which eventually became the most important theatrical company in the country. He was also director of the Escuela de Teatro at the Instituto de Bellas Artes in Cali.

Buenaventura developed a "method of collective work" for the theatre in which the actors participated in the writing of a play. Influenced politically by Marxist theories, his works emphasize social criticism, as can be seen in the *Schoolteacher*, where the peasants are victimized by the oligarchy and government officials. In other instances we see the vision of Bertolt Brecht, as in *The Orgy*, where the actors speak directly to (or point at) members of the audience, thus making them participants in the drama.

THE ORGY

CHARACTERS:

The Old Woman
The Mute
1st Beggar
2nd Beggar
3rd Beggar
The Dwarf

Sitting in a very old easy chair in front of a mirror, the Old Woman primps. On both sides of the chair are two piles of clothing that had once been lovely and elegant.

OLD WOMAN: How could I possibly know where you hid it! You always hide it in the strangest places, and then you accuse me of stealing it. It's always the same thing! God, our heavenly Father, who is on high and can see everything we do, knows I don't steal your money! Who knows where you stuck it, you greedy little pig! Your greed is eating you up. *(A pause. She starts to primp again. Her son, a mute, grunts furiously. He looks everywhere. Then he turns to the audience and makes motions, accusing his mother of stealing the money he earns from shining shoes.)*
Besides, even if I spend a few cents, I'm not stealing them. I have the right to spend them, because I gave birth to you, and I raised and supported every inch of you. I'm your mother. *(The Mute turns to her and asks again for the money.)*
What's wrong with you is that you're jealous. You're jealous! Jealous... jealous; jealousy is going to eat you up. How long has it been? Oh, forget about that money! Listen to me! Oh, how could he hear, anyway? He's as deaf as a post! This is my punishment from God! How long has it been? Thirty... forty years. Forty-five? Forty-seven, maybe... You looked exactly the same then as you do now; you were born that way. *(The Mute makes indications that she has stolen thirty-five dollars from him.)*
Thirty-five! That's not true. I took twenty miserable dollars for the Orgy of the Thirtieth. Twenty miserable dollars. You liar! Now he's going to say that he's the one who supports me! If it wasn't for

the generosity of those people, that's right, of those people you hate, those people who make you so jealous, I would die all alone in this hovel. *(A pause. She begins to primp again. The Mute grunts in an impotent rage. He makes signs that he would like to kill her, that he would like to wring her neck.)*

You would, too. You would. *(A pause. She continues to primp; she ostentatiously combs her gray hair.)*

How long has it been? Fifty years? Has it been fifty already? I didn't steal thirty-five dollars from you. I took twenty for the Orgy of the Thirtieth. Today is orgy day. And don't you say one word to me. You talk too much. *(A pause.)* How could he talk? He's as dumb as a doorknob. *(A pause.)* Look at your father there. *(The Mute smiles beatifically. He feels a great veneration for his father. He looks at the picture. His rage melts away.)*

He was the gabbiest man in the world. How his moustache used to move... In fact, I sometimes get the feeling it's still moving. *(The Mute grunts.)* You're even jealous of him. How long has it been? Let's say it was exactly forty years ago. *(She starts to do an actual striptease as she talks. She takes off clothes that are so old they're about to fall apart.)*

The prince who was to be king kissed my hand on the train in Argentina. Come on, come on, help me. Do it for your father! He loved this story!

(She caresses him. That calms him down, and he begins to help her.) You're there. We're on the train. *(The Mute smiles. He likes the train. He imitates it.)*

We can see the Pampa through the window. The whole Pampa! This is the prince's first trip to South America. He's in my compartment. Straighten up! The prince looks like he's swallowed an umbrella! Come to attention! The prince looks like he has a pea stuck up his ass. *(She pulls back her hand that the Mute is clumsily trying to kiss. The Mute clutches desperately at the hand, struggling to kiss it.)*

Stop it! Stop it, you imbecile! Now you're just trying to flatter me! You greedy thing! *(The Mute becomes furious. He grabs hold of a pot that's on the table, backstage.)*

Our food. Leave the food for the orgy there: I bought it with my money. With my money. Mine! Oh, my God! God, why did you give me this punishment? I'm paying for my sins with him, Lord! Mea culpa! Mea culpa! Mea fucking culpa! *(The Mute lets go of the pot and goes to her. He kneels down beside her. He crosses himself amid tender*

THE ORGY

grunts. He lays his head in her lap. He pushes against her, as though wanting to return to the womb. She caresses him. She smiles.)

You'd like to get back in there, wouldn't you? You'd like to curl back up inside here again. *(She touches her stomach.)* And when you were there, you used to kick, trying to get out. That's just like a man! They spend nine months, struggling to get out, and all their lives fighting to get back in. *(She laughs so hard that tears come to her eyes.)* All right, all right, calm down. Don't hug me so tight that you wake up the devil in me. Instead of being so loving you should be more generous. Get up. Don't grunt. You have to go to Jacob's and to Peter's and... Stop your growling and grunting. Let's have no jealousy here. There's nothing here any longer, my dear. I don't get aroused now. My poor flame has burned itself out. It doesn't even smolder any more. And their flames have all gone cold too. Peter's, John's, Jacob's, Anthony's, and the ones who are dead too, may they rest in peace. What you used to watch through the cracks doesn't exist anymore. Oh, you little rascal. You used to like to look at your mother. You liked to see these things, didn't you? I know that you hate these men, but you have to go to them and pry money out of them. Since you're such a greedy fellow, I have to beg them to help. I'm a beggar too! Like my own beggars! Like my beggars from the Orgy of the Thirtieth. The ones you hate. *(The Mute makes signs that she's wasting money on these disgusting people. He spits on them, actually spitting toward the audience.)*

It's my money; I earned it. I earned it when I was myself, and I still earn it for old times' sake. *(He makes signs, indicating that that is not true, that she steals it all from him. He turns his pockets inside out to indicate what she does to him.)*

You're a greedy pig, a goddam greedy little pig. Yes, I spend money on those beggars—I have fun with the beggars. I have a right to enjoy myself. Go on, get out and make some money. Go shine the shoes of the whole world. You despicable thing, get out! *(She threatens him with a broom. The Mute runs off, laughing and playing with her. The Old Woman sits down on her decrepit old chair, exhausted. A pause.)*

Jacob is that you? The prince who was to be King of England took his first trip to South America back at the time of the first war. And his last trip too. How could you want him to come to this horrible South America we have now? We were on the same train. I had a whole compartment all to myself... You could see the Pampa through the windows… the train… Little money, not much money, little money, not much money. *(She goes faster and faster until she ends in convulsions.)* But that cost… *(She begins quickly, and gradually slows down to a complete stop.)* Lots of money, loads of money, lots of money, loads of money… Shshshshshshshsh… *(As though the engine were letting off steam.)*

1ST BEGGAR: Lord be praised.

OLD WOMAN: Did you get here all right? Where were you, you scabby son of a bitch?

1ST BEGGAR: I don't feel so good… my chest… *(He coughs. He spits into a bloody rag.)*

OLD WOMAN: Don't act so pompous. You don't have any right to get such a delicate illness. In my time that was a very distinguished illness. Now everybody's uncle has it.

1ST BEGGAR: If I could get something to eat at these Orgies of the Thirtieth, I'd feel a lot better. At least, once a month!

OLD WOMAN: Well, this is a spiritual observance. A memorial. I won't allow it to be dirtied by the materialism of these days.

1ST BEGGAR: Today I'm charging a dollar thirty.

OLD WOMAN: Why?

1ST BEGGAR: I live further away. I have to take a bus.

OLD WOMAN: Jacob used to ride in a carriage. A big horse-drawn carriage.

1ST BEGGAR: Who?

OLD WOMAN: Get dressed. *(The beggar, who is nearly skin and bones, takes off his clothes. He shivers. He pulls an old, fancily-decorated shirt from one of the piles of clothes, and puts it on. He coughs.)* Don't you go and get Jacob's clothes dirty. *(The beggar puts on a moth-eaten jacket. Pants. Everything is too big for him. He puts on the top hat, but he can't get the gloves on. His fingers are all bent and twisted from arthritis.)* Jacob, you've grown smaller… Oh, my dear, bring me a chair. Pull that curtain open; I can't see very well. Hand me the binoculars. My God, you old scab! Stick your gloves up your ass, but don't keep twisting them around, trying to put them on… You're going to make me dizzy!

1ST BEGGAR: They don't fit.

OLD WOMAN: Don't talk.

1ST BEGGAR *(Enraged)*: But I can't get them on.

OLD WOMAN: Shut up.

THE ORGY

1ST BEGGAR: Don't shout at me. *(He throws down the gloves.)*

OLD WOMAN: Do you want to leave here without the orgy? Do you want to lose your alms? *(She shouts.)*

1ST BEGGAR *(Humiliated):* No. No, Ma'am.

OLD WOMAN: Pick up your gloves! *(The Beggar picks up his gloves, and goes into a fit of coughing.)* Don't cough! *(The Beggar struggles to stop coughing.)*

1ST BEGGAR: What… *(He starts coughing again; he holds it back.)* I've got to cough!

OLD WOMAN: Hold it back.

1ST BEGGAR *(With a great effort):* I've got tu-ber-cu-lo-sis.

OLD WOMAN: Don't talk about that. *(A short pause.)* Start in. I'm anxious to get started. *(A pause.)* While we wait for the others to get here.

1ST BEGGAR: You want me to start?

OLD WOMAN: Go ahead.

1ST BEGGAR *(He takes a deep bow):* How beautiful you are, Maria Cristina. *(He has a fit of coughing in order to cover up his laughter.)*

OLD WOMAN: Don't cough.

1ST BEGGAR: Listen to the way my chest sounds. *(His chest rumbles.)*

OLD WOMAN: Dear Jacob, pull up that chair for me. And draw back that curtain; I can't see very well. Hand me the binoculars. *(She looks at the audience through the pair of rickety binoculars that the Beggar hands her.)* Look. There they are. And every one of them with his little private life all under lock and key… They've come here *not* to see. They don't want to see. That's why they come. If they could see they'd be frightened. Do you think they're dead? No. That one over there just moved. Old what's-his-name. What's-her-name supports him and she's so and so's mistress. Look at that one. *(She whispers animatedly in his ear. They both laugh.)* Look at her, over there. *(She hands him the binoculars. He looks. He gives the binoculars back to her and whispers at great length into her ear. He talks so long that he chokes and starts coughing.)* You goddam pig, turn your head away when you cough! *(She looks through the binoculars.)* And that one, that one there!—Oh, that one over there! *(She whispers in the Beggar's ear. The two start laughing louder and louder. The Beggar points to someone in the audience, and they burst into shrieks of laughter. Suddenly the Old Woman's laughter breaks off, and she pulls the Beggar's arm down.)*

Don't point. They're starting to notice. *(She motions the Beggar to stoop down so she can tell him a secret. He bends over. She whispers the secret to him. He nods his head. He looks through the binoculars and whispers into her ear. The game begins to move faster. They pass the binoculars back and forth very quickly and say things in a jumble. 2nd Beggar comes in.)*

2ND BEGGAR: 'Evening.

OLD WOMAN: Don't interrupt. We're at the theatre. *(2nd Beggar pretends to become interested. He looks at the audience.)*

2ND BEGGAR: What are they performing?

OLD WOMAN: Their own lives. *(She points at the audience.)*

2ND BEGGAR: How is it?

OLD WOMAN: Boring. Get dressed. It's your turn to play Peter today.

2ND BEGGAR: From now on I'm going to charge a dollar fifty for the Orgies of the Thirtieth.

OLD WOMAN *(To 1st Beggar):* What an interesting play. The best one I've seen. Look. *(They start the game again, but more slowly this time.)* Oh, Jacob, gossip excites me so. *(1st Beggar whispers at length into her ear. In the meantime the 2nd Beggar undresses. Under his ragged clothing he has on an old prisoner's uniform. He puts on a large silk coat over it, and a ragged top hat. The 1st Beggar is still whispering in the Old Woman's ear.)* That one? *(She points. The 1st Beggar moves her hand.)* Oh, that one? *(He moves her hand. The Old Woman gets up.)* Oh, oh, that one, that one. *(He moves her hand. They both move forward, toward the audience.)* Oh, that one? *(He moves her hand. They move even closer.)* This one then? *(He moves her hand. They reach the edge of the stage.)* This one. *(The Old Woman pulls back her hand, as though her finger had been burned.)* We're pointing. Do you think they've noticed? No? *(She looks out tenderly at the audience.)* They haven't noticed. They're so innocent…

2ND BEGGAR: I said that from now on I'm going to charge a dollar fifty for each Orgy of the Thirtieth.

OLD WOMAN *(To 1st Beggar):* Wash out your mouth once in a while, you scabby old thing. It's nothing but a sewer. *(To 2nd Beggar.)* The others aren't here yet.

2ND BEGGAR: If you aren't going to pay, then I'm going to take off these clothes. *(He makes a motion as though he's going to undress.)*

1ST BEGGAR: That's a lot of money, Ma'am. He's taking advantage of you.

2ND BEGGAR: You suck-ass!

OLD WOMAN: That lazy bunch of good-for-nothings. Those scabby old bums. I always have to wait for them.

2ND BEGGAR: Then I'm getting out of these clothes. *(He takes off his coat.)*

OLD WOMAN: You goddam ungrateful bastard. Who got you out of jail? Who do you owe your freedom to? How much is your freedom worth?

2ND BEGGAR: I live a long way from here. I get here all out of breath… and then…

OLD WOMAN: Then what?

2ND BEGGAR: Then the food gets worse at every orgy…

OLD WOMAN: Can't you people think about anything besides eating? Is food the only thing you live for? Don't spiritual things mean anything to you? That's why this country is in the shape it's in. Because the only thing anybody thinks about is eating.

1ST BEGGAR: That's true, Ma'am. *(To 2nd Beggar.)* All you think about is eating.

2ND BEGGAR: It's because my stomach always hurts.

1ST BEGGAR: He's so materialistic, Ma'am. *(To 2nd Beggar.)* I'm asking for a dollar thirty, and I have to take the bus.

2ND BEGGAR *(Going up to him)*: You poor thing. Do you want me to tell some other things about you?

1ST BEGGAR: Ma'am, we're at the theatre. *(He looks at the audience through the binoculars.)*

2ND BEGGAR: You Jesuit.

OLD WOMAN: All right, let's cut out the squabbling. I'll raise the alms of the Orgy of the Thirtieth to a dollar twenty, but not one cent more.

1ST BEGGAR: The bus costs thirty cents, and it's going to go up to forty.

OLD WOMAN: A dollar twenty, and no more.

2ND BEGGAR: That's exploitation.

1ST BEGGAR *(To 2nd Beggar)*: You lost it all. I already had my dollar thirty.

OLD WOMAN: If you don't like it, I'll get some other beggars. They're like this. *(She opens and closes the fingers of her right hand to indicate how many there are.)* We're swarming with them.

2ND BEGGAR: Pure exploitation.

OLD WOMAN: And the others still aren't here.

2ND BEGGAR: If we can all agree on this…

ENRIQUE BUENAVENTURA

OLD WOMAN: Everyone knows that it's on the thirtieth of every month. The thirtieth. Every month has thirty…
1ST BEGGAR: We should have agreed on it before. The only one that doesn't have thirty is August, and it has thirty-one.
2ND BEGGAR: And every time she gives us less food. What does she do with the leftovers? Why doesn't she put out all the food?
OLD WOMAN: Nobody can forget the thirtieth.
1ST BEGGAR: She gets crazier every time we get together.
OLD WOMAN: Thirty miserable beggars.
2ND BEGGAR: Thirty thirsty thieves…
1ST BEGGAR: Thrashing through the thorny thicket. *(They laugh.)*
OLD WOMAN: On every thirtieth of the month.
1ST BEGGAR *(Keeping up the joke)*: Today is the 29th. There's only twenty-nine days in a month.
OLD WOMAN: And what happens to the thirtieth? *(The Beggars shrug.)* In other countries I've been to—even Argentina—all the months have thirty days. But since this country is full of thieves, they steal the thirtieth from some months.
2ND BEGGAR: They stole the thirtieth today.
1ST BEGGAR: And this is the twenty-ninth.
OLD WOMAN: Then not everybody will come.
2ND BEGGAR: All the better. There'll be more for us to eat.
1ST BEGGAR: We could take the lid off the pot.
OLD WOMAN: Jacob, remember that you have a very small appetite.
1ST BEGGAR: Who?
OLD WOMAN: You.
1ST BEGGAR: Me?
OLD WOMAN: Yes.
1ST BEGGAR: I didn't know that.
OLD WOMAN: You're Jacob today, and Jacob never ate very much. He was a gentleman.
1ST BEGGAR: A gentleman with no appetite… What a goddam waste.
OLD WOMAN: Set the table. *(The beggars jump to get the pot.)* I said the table; I didn't say to bring the pot. Put it back.
1ST BEGGAR: But, Ma'am
2ND BEGGAR: I haven't had a bite to eat since yesterday.
OLD WOMAN: I said the table.
1ST BEGGAR: Please.

THE ORGY

2ND BEGGAR: Get real, damn it.

1ST BEGGAR: A crumb for a poor, starving old man. *(He takes the lid off the pot.)*

OLD WOMAN: Put the lid back on the pot.

2ND BEGGAR: *(He puts in his hand and pulls something out, quickly putting it in his mouth.)*

OLD WOMAN: You goddam pig.

2ND BEGGAR *(With his mouth full):* Mmm. Mmm... mmmmm. *(He indicates that he is hungry.)*

OLD WOMAN: You thief. You thief. *(She runs after him with a stick. Meanwhile the 1st Beggar puts his hand into the pot and starts stuffing his mouth. The Old Woman throws down the stick and goes over to the table. She picks up a knife and stands next to the pot.)* If either one of you comes one step closer I'll send his soul packing.

1ST BEGGAR: My soul is very weak, Ma'am.

2ND BEGGAR: I ate mine quite a while back.

1ST BEGGAR: Don't make such a big thing out of it, Ma'am. Remember, I'm Jacob. *(He straightens his clothing.)*

2ND BEGGAR: And I'm Peter. *(He does the same.)* How were Peter's grinders, Ma'am?

OLD WOMAN *(Going along with the game):* He was toothless.

2ND BEGGAR: Like me. But I have gums as hard as a rock.

OLD WOMAN *(With the knife in her belt):* Put the flowers on the table. *(They bring out a jug with old, decrepit artificial flowers. The Old Woman starts playing the game again.)* Colonel Gray sent them to me this morning. Aren't they beautiful? Smell them.

2ND BEGGAR *(Going along with the joke):* What an aroma.

OLD WOMAN *(To the 2nd Beggar):* You smell them, sir.

2ND BEGGAR: They're roses.

OLD WOMAN: They're fuchsias.

2ND BEGGAR: I mean fuchsias.

OLD WOMAN *(Remembering, caught up):* Colonel Gray always used to send me fuchsias. *(3rd Beggar enters.)* Colonel! *(Her hand is trembling. The Beggar hesitates for a second. The other two Beggars are dying with laughter. The 3rd Beggar kisses her hand. She turns away in disgust.)* What made you so late? You goddam pig. Hurry up and get dressed. Put on the uniform. Today you're Colonel Gray. The full-dress uniform. *(The 3rd Beggar begins to rummage through the pile of clothes.)* Law and order are here. If you don't keep order and discipline, you'll lose

your alms and the orgies of the thirtieth each month.
1ST BEGGAR: But every time we meet we get less to eat.
2ND BEGGAR: Last month there was a lot left over,
OLD WOMAN: There always have to be leftovers.
1ST BEGGAR: Why?
OLD WOMAN: Because there's a lot of food.
2ND BEGGAR: And what do you do with the leftovers?
OLD WOMAN: I throw them, I fling them away, I pitch them out... like this.
1ST BEGGAR: Where do you throw them?
OLD WOMAN: Jacob!
1ST BEGGAR: Damn Jacob to Hell! I want the leftovers!
OLD WOMAN: Shut up, you mangy old animal. If you start in again, it's all over for you, and you'll never get back in here again. Colonel, I have a lot of complaints for you about these two.
3RD BEGGAR: You ought to throw him out, Ma'am. He's nothing but a lousy bastard.
2ND BEGGAR: Or not let him into the orgies of the thirtieth. The members of the orgies ought to be chosen very carefully.
1ST BEGGAR: You sons of bitches! *(He throws down his gloves.)*
OLD WOMAN: Shut up. Pick up your gloves, Jacob. Are you ready, Colonel?
3RD BEGGAR: Yes, Ma'am, but I wanted to tell you
OLD WOMAN: No, no, no. Don't tell us again.
3RD BEGGAR: ...that the orgies...
OLD WOMAN: Don't tell us again.
3RD BEGGAR: ...are really cheap. I mean, Ma'am... I mean, a dollar isn't much for an orgy... I was thinking...
OLD WOMAN: We don't want to know how you lost your leg in the Thousand Days' War... There are so many versions. But it's the ten thousandth time you've told it, Colonel... How did it happen?
3RD BEGGAR: I don't want to make out that I'm a big shot, but I've got something that's really good for orgies, Ma'am. I'm missing a leg. That's something not everybody can say.
OLD WOMAN: Your leg. Your precious leg that's on the country's altar. Lying there. Along with the other ideals. *(A brief pause.)* Rotten, stinking, full of worms. It's disgusting.
3RD BEGGAR *(Shouting)*: No, Ma'am. It's something... something special. If you won't pay me two dollars for the orgy, my leg won't

THE ORGY

work. *(A pause. An awkward silence.)*

1ST BEGGAR: It went up to one twenty. She won't give a penny more.

2ND BEGGAR: Either we all get more money, or none of us gets any.

3RD BEGGAR: You two have both your legs.

OLD WOMAN: All right, it's over. You can all get out of here. This is an orgy of art and memories, it's not something commercial. Do whatever you want to. I can get other beggars. I have a lot of them who want to join. Right out there. *(She repeats the gesture with her fingers.)* They're just swarming all over the place. *(The beggars huddle into a conference. A pause.)*

3RD BEGGAR *(Coming to attention)*: Ma'am! I'm ready.

OLD WOMAN: Your leg, your tired old leg... How did it get up and start to walk away all by itself?

3RD BEGGAR: I was marching along at the head of the liberal forces. I was carrying the red flag, and it was waving and waving in the breeze.

OLD WOMAN: Fluttering, you say fluttering.

3RD BEGGAR: Fluttering. And there, up in front of us, were the damn conservatives.

2ND BEGGAR: Don't you start saying bad things about the conservatives. I won't allow it, Ma'am. He's always using the orgies of the thirtieth for political purposes.

3RD BEGGAR: The fuckin' conservatives, those goddam, high and mighty conservatives...

2ND BEGGAR: I won't allow it, Ma'am. I won't put up with it. Do you want to lose another leg? *(The 1st Beggar is shaking with laughter.)* Do you want to lose another leg? *(He pulls out a knife, presses the button, and the blade flies open.)* Do you want another wooden stick full of termites on the other side? *(The 3rd Beggar pulls a dagger from his crutches.)*

OLD WOMAN: I just adore political battles. *(To the 1st Beggar.)* Jacob, what are you?

1ST BEGGAR *(Breaking off his laughter, and crossing himself)*: A Christian. *(The female Dwarf enters.)*

DWARF: Ooh hoo hooo: Here I am! *(A pause. Silence. The Dwarf looks at everyone.)* Did the orgy begin yet? *(The two Beggars slowly put away their weapons. The Dwarf turns to the Old Woman.)* I got here late because today's not the thirtieth; it's the twenty-ninth. But I asked this morning at church, and they told me it was the end of the month. But it's not the thirtieth, I said. It's leap year, they told me. Then I came.

OLD WOMAN: And now, my story.

2ND BEGGAR: It's already been told ten jillion times.

1ST BEGGAR: You were on the train.

OLD WOMAN *(Carried away):* Yes.

2ND BEGGAR: You could see the Pampa out the window.

OLD WOMAN: Yes. *(A pause.)* There it is.

1ST BEGGAR: Out there in the Pampa *(He points to the audience.)* the sun hasn't come up yet. It's still dark.

DWARF: Should I get dressed?

OLD WOMAN: Yes.

DWARF: What should I dress as?

OLD WOMAN: Anything. The Bishop, if you want.

DWARF: Oh, yes! The Bishop! *(She begins to get dressed.)*

3RD BEGGAR: The prince who was to be king of England…

1ST BEGGAR: …was taking his first and last trip through South America.

2ND BEGGAR: He was on the train…

OLD WOMAN: Little money, not much money, little money, not much money…

3RD BEGGAR: You had an entire compartment all to yourself.

OLD WOMAN *(Speeding up):* Little money, not much money, little money, not much money…

1ST BEGGAR *(Raising his voice):* And then the prince who was to be king…

OLD WOMAN *(Like background music):* Little money, not much money, little money, not much money, little money, not much money…

2ND BEGGAR: He came to your apartment and…

3RD BEGGAR: He kissed your hand! *(He kisses her hand.)*

OLD WOMAN: Ohhh. *(This cry is the signal for the orgy to begin. The 1st Beggar grabs an untuned guitar and begins to play. They all dance. The Old Woman passes around the bottle and everyone takes a drink. The Dwarf puts the pot on the table and everyone rushes over to eat.)* Just a minute. Another drink and another dance. *(They pass around the bottle. They take enormous swigs, and they dance. The Dwarf and the Old Woman raise their skirts and the Beggars fondle them. The women affect prudishness. The Old Woman pushes away the 2nd Beggar as he puts his hand around her waist.)*

THE ORGY

2ND BEGGAR: That's enough: let's eat.

1ST BEGGAR: Let's eat.

3RD BEGGAR: It's time to eat.

DWARF: I'll serve. *(She says the blessing.)* In nomine Patris, et Filium…

OLD WOMAN: All right, that's enough. Pass the bottle, you filthy little midget. Let's drink freely and eat moderately, like ladies and gentlemen. This is a decent orgy.

1ST BEGGAR: It's getting harder and harder to eat at these friggin' orgies.

OLD WOMAN: Come here, Jacob. You're the Governor. You here, Mr. Mayor. You tell me how the Government is doing. *(The 1st Beggar gives a very complicated pantomime of how the Government is doing.)* I don't understand a bit of it, and I'm laughing. *(She laughs very theatrically.)*

DWARF: I'm at the Government's side. Dominus, Dominus…

OLD WOMAN: Jacob, give your speech.

DWARF: Dominus, Dominus, Dominus. *(She goes on as background music.)*

OLD WOMAN: Speak, Mr. Governor, we're waiting.

1ST BEGGAR *(Standing on the chair, with the pathetic tone and gestures of a very serious political leader)*: I would like something to eat.

BEGGARS: Hooray!

OLD WOMAN: He's always such a demagogue! *(The other Beggars applaud.)*

1ST BEGGAR: We ought to be able to eat all we want at these damn orgies of the thirtieth. I ask you, ladies and gentlemen: Why can't we eat? Why do we have to go hungry when the meal is sitting here? What is the answer to this riddle, ladies and gentlemen? Who can solve it? My stomach is stuck against my spine, we're starving like dogs, the meal is sitting here, and we can't even move our little fingers! Let's have something to eat at these orgies of the thirtieth! *(He has a coughing fit.)*

OLD WOMAN: One of the best speeches from one of the best governors at one of the best orgies.

2ND BEGGAR: It's not right for there to be leftovers.

3RD BEGGAR AND DWARF: No! It's not right!

OLD WOMAN: Even the masses are getting stirred up!

DWARF: Christ gave out the loaves of bread and the fish and the frijoles and the tortillas.

ENRIQUE BUENAVENTURA

1ST BEGGAR: We want the leftovers.
2ND BEGGAR: We want the leftovers.
DWARF: We want the leftovers.
3RD BEGGAR: We want the leftovers.
ALL THE BEGGARS: We want the leftovers! We want it all!
1ST BEGGAR *(Taking the lid off the pot)*: All!
OLD WOMAN: Let's stop this right now! I'll give out the food when I get good and ready! *(She grabs hold of the pot.)*
2ND BEGGAR: Let go of that pot!
3RD BEGGAR: You stingy old bitch!
OLD WOMAN *(Struggling)*: You animals! You filthy drunks! You're all full of shit. Get back. *(For a second the Beggars move back. The Dwarf, still standing behind her, tries to reach the pot with her cane. The Old Woman picks up a knife. The Dwarf moves back.)* You're nothing but a pile of crap. You aren't my gentlemen. You just take advantage of a helpless old lady who has only a mute son.
2ND BEGGAR *(Advancing toward her)*: The play is over! The play is over!
3RD BEGGAR: You crazy old lady! You crazy old lady!
OLD WOMAN *(Throwing the knife)*: Get back, you stinking pile of shit.
1ST BEGGAR: You old murderer. You stabbed me. You stabbed me.
2ND BEGGAR: You murderer.
DWARF: Ooh hoo hee! Let's have the orgy. *(She hits the Old Woman over the head with her cane. The Old Woman falls back onto the table. The Beggars fall on her, beat and stab her. She lies sprawled out on the table. Her head hangs down and her grey hair touches the floor. Silently, the Beggars devour the meal. The 1st Beggar starts to leave.)*
2ND BEGGAR: Where are you going?
1ST BEGGAR: To piss.
2ND BEGGAR: You're lying.
3RD BEGGAR: You're going out to look for the Mute's money.
DWARF *(To the corpse of the Old Woman)*: Ego te absolvo in nomini Patris, et Filium, et Spiritu Sancti...
2ND BEGGAR: Let's get out of these clothes and we'll all go looking for it. *(They take off their costumes and put on their ragged old clothes again.)*
1ST BEGGAR: She was crazy as a loon.
2ND BEGGAR: They say the Mute has a lot of money hidden somewhere. He's been hoarding it for thirty years.
3RD BEGGAR: That's not true. She stole it all from him.

THE ORGY

1ST BEGGAR: Someone stand guard while we look for the money.

DWARF: Requiet canti in pace. Amen.

2ND BEGGAR: Let the Dwarf stand guard. *(They lift her up to the table and she pretends to be looking through a window.)*

DWARF: Here comes the Mute. *(The Beggars run out, followed by the Dwarf. The Mute enters, counting his money. He sees the Old Woman, runs over to her and lifts up her head. Then he goes to the front of the stage and asks the audience why, why did all this happen... Why?)*

BLACKOUT

THE SCHOOLTEACHER

ENRIQUE BUENAVENTURA

ENRIQUE BUENAVENTURA

CHARACTERS:

The Teacher
Juana Pasambú
Pedro Pasambú
Squint-eyed Tobias
Old Asunción
Sergeant
Peregrino Pasambú

A young woman is seated on a bench, downstage. Behind her, or to her side, certain scenes will take place. There should be no direct interaction between her and the characters in those scenes. She doesn't see them, and they don't see her.

THE TEACHER: I am dead. I was born here, in this town. In the little house made of red clay, with a straw roof. By the road, across from the school. The road is a slow moving river of red clay in winter, and a whirlwind of red dust in summer. When the rains come you lose your sandals in the mud, the mules and horses get their bellies smeared with mud, the saddles and even the faces of the horsemen are spattered with mud. In the months when the sun hangs high and long in the sky, the entire town is covered with red dirt. The sandals go up the road, filled with red dirt, and the hooves and legs of the horses, and the snorting nostrils of the mules and horses, and the manes, and saddles, and the sweaty faces, and hats, all become filled with red dirt. I was born from that mud, and from that red dirt, and now I have returned to it. Here, in the small cemetery that watches over the town below, surrounded by daisies, geraniums, lilies, and thick grass. The acrid smell of red mud mingles with the sweet odor of *yaraguá* grass, and in the afternoon even the smell of the woods drifts overhead, and rushes down upon the town. *(A pause.)* They brought me here in the evening. *(A funeral procession, upstage, with a coffin.)* Juana Pasambú, my aunt, came.

THE SCHOOLTEACHER

JUANA PASAMBU: Why didn't you eat?

THE TEACHER: I wouldn't eat. Why eat? Food had no meaning anymore. You eat to live, and I didn't want to live. Life no longer had meaning. Pedro Pasambú, my uncle, came.

PEDRO PASAMBU: You liked bananas and corn on the cob with salt and butter.

THE TEACHER: I liked bananas and corn on the cob, but I wouldn't eat them. I kept my mouth tightly closed. *(A pause.)* Squint-eyed Tobias is here: he was the mayor years ago.

SQUINT-EYED TOBIAS: I brought you water from the spring where you drank when you were a little girl; I brought it in a cup made of leaves, and you wouldn't drink it.

THE TEACHER: I didn't want to drink. I kept my lips pressed together. God forgive me, I began to wish the spring would dry up. Why did water continue to gush out of the spring? I wondered. For what reason? *(A pause.)* Old Asunción was here. The midwife who brought me into the world.

OLD ASUNCION: Oh, woman! Oh, my child! I brought you into this world. Oh, my baby! Why wouldn't you take anything from my hands? Why did you spit out the soup I gave you? My hands that have healed so many, why couldn't they heal your torn flesh? And while the murderers were here... *(The people in the funeral procession look around with terror. The old woman continues her mute wailing while the teacher speaks.)*

THE TEACHER: They are afraid. Some time ago fear came to this town and hung suspended over it like a great storm cloud. The air reeks of fear, voices dissolve in the bitter spittle of fear, and the people swallow it. Yesterday the cloud ripped open, and the thunderbolt fell upon us.

The funeral procession disappears. A violent roll of drums is heard in the darkness. When the light comes on again, where the procession was there is now an old farmer, on his knees, his hands tied behind his back. In front of him stands a police sergeant.

SERGEANT *(Looking at a list):* Your name's Peregrino Pasambú, right? *(The old man nods.)* Then you're the big honcho here. *(The old man shakes his head.)*

THE TEACHER: Father had been named mayor twice by the government. But he understood so little about politics that he didn't realize the government had changed.

SERGEANT: You got this land because of politics, right?

THE TEACHER: That wasn't true. My father was one of the founders of the town. And because he was one of the founders he had this house next to the road, with some land. He gave the town its name. He called it "Hope."

SERGEANT: Aren't you gonna talk? Aren't you gonna say anything?

THE TEACHER: My father didn't talk much.

SERGEANT: This land ain't divided right. We're gonna divide it all over again. It's gonna have real owners, with deeds and everything.

THE TEACHER: When my father came here, it was all a jungle.

SERGEANT: The jobs haven't been given out too good, either. Your daughter's the schoolteacher, ain't she?

THE TEACHER: It wasn't really a job. They seldom paid me my salary. But I liked to be the schoolteacher. My mother was the first teacher the school ever had. She taught me, and when she died I became the teacher.

SERGEANT: Who knows what that dame teaches.

THE TEACHER: I taught reading and writing, and I taught catechism, and love for our country and our flag. When I refused to eat and drink, I thought about the children. It was true that there weren't very many of them, but who was going to teach them? And then I thought: why should they learn the catechism? Why should they learn to love their country and their flag? Country and flag don't mean anything anymore. Maybe it wasn't right, but that's what I thought.

SERGEANT: Why don't you talk? This ain't my doing. I'm not to blame. I'm just following orders. *(He shouts.)* You see this list? All the big chiefs and fat cats of the last government are on it. We got orders to get rid of them all so we can set up the elections. *(The sergeant and the old man disappear.)*

THE TEACHER: So that's the way it was. They put him against the mud wall behind the house. The sergeant gave the order, and the soldiers shot. Then the sergeant and the soldiers came into my room and, one after another, they raped me. Then I wouldn't eat or drink again, and so I died, little by little. Little by little. Now it will rain soon, and the red dirt will turn to mud. The road will be a slow moving river of red mud, and the sandals will come up the road

THE SCHOOLTEACHER

again, and the mud covered feet, and the horses and mules with their bellies full of mud, and even the faces and the hats will go up the road, splattered with mud.

THE END

THE STORY OF THE MAN WHO TURNED INTO A DOG

OSVALDO DRAGÚN

OSVALDO DRAGÚN

OSVALDO DRAGÚN

Argentina: 1929-1999

Dragún was born in Colonia Becerro, a Jewish agricultural settlement, to a family that had fled the pogroms of Russia. His parents later relocated to Buenos Aires, where he attended school, studying law at the university. However, he abandoned his studies and joined the Fray Mocho Theatre in 1956. While with that group, he wrote his much performed *Historias para ser contadas* (Tales to Be Told).

In 1966 a political coup d'état brought in a regime opposed to independent theatres, and Dragún began to spend time abroad, directing plays in other Latin American countries and in the United States. By 1980, artistic repression had eased, and Dragún and other playwrights formed an "Argentina Open Theatre," a theatrical collective to protect themselves from being blacklisted by the dictatorship. He also worked in Cuba and in Mexico, returning to Argentina in 1996 to become director of the Teatro Cervantes. In addition, he wrote scripts for television and feature films.

His dramas often reflect the influence of Brecht in making the audience aware that they are watching the artifice of theatre. The plays included here are part of his *Historias para ser contadas*, and depict the themes of social injustice that so preoccupied him.

THE STORY OF THE MAN WHO TURNED INTO A DOG

CHARACTERS:

1st Actor
2nd Actor
3rd Actor
Actress

2ND ACTOR: Friends, we're going to tell the story this way.
3RD ACTOR: Just the way they told it to us this afternoon.
ACTRESS: It's the "Story of the Man Who Turned into a Dog."
3RD ACTOR: It began two years ago on a park bench. There, sir... where you were trying to discover the secret of a leaf.
ACTRESS: There, where we stretch out our arms and hold the world tightly by its head and feet, and we tell it: "Play, accordion, play!"
2ND ACTOR: We met him there. *(1st Actor enters.)* He was... *(He points to him.)* just like that—the way you see him there. And he was very sad.
ACTRESS: He was our friend. He was looking for a job, and we were actors.
3RD ACTOR: He had to support his wife, and we were actors.
2ND ACTOR: He dreamed about life, and woke up screaming at night. And we were actors.
ACTRESS: He was a close friend of ours, of course. Just the way you see him there... *(She points to him.)* No different.
EVERYONE: And he was so sad!
3RD ACTOR: Time passed. Autumn...
2ND ACTOR: Summer...
ACTRESS: Winter...
3RD ACTOR: Spring...
1ST ACTOR: That's a lie! I never had a springtime.
2ND ACTOR: Autumn...
ACTRESS: Winter...
3RD ACTOR: Summer. And we came back. And we went to visit him, because he was our friend.
2ND ACTOR: And we asked: "Is he all right?" And his wife told us...
ACTRESS: I don't know.

OSVALDO DRAGÚN

3RD ACTOR: Is he sick?
ACTRESS: I don't know.
2ND AND 3RD ACTORS: Where is he?
ACTRESS: In the doghouse. *(The 1st Actor gets down on all fours.)*
2ND AND 3RD ACTORS: Oooh!
3RD ACTOR *(Watching him):*
I am in charge of the doghouse,
And this seems most curious to me.
When he came here he barked like a dog
(the primary requisite, you see);
Though he still wears the clothes of a human,
He's a dog, it's as plain as can be.
2ND ACTOR *(Stuttering):*
I-I-I am the v-v-veterinarian,
And th-th-this is qu-quite clear t-to me.
Alth-th-though he m-may look like a m-man,
He's a d-d-dog, th-this fellow you see.
1ST ACTOR *(To the audience):* As for me, what can I tell you? I don't know if I'm a man or a dog. And, when all's said and done, I don't think even you could tell me. It all began in the most ordinary way. I went to a factory, looking for a job. I hadn't been able to find anything for three months, and I went there, looking for work.
3RD ACTOR: Didn't you read the sign? "No Help Wanted."
1ST ACTOR: Yes, I read it. Don't you have anything for me?
3RD ACTOR: If it says "No Help Wanted," there isn't anything.
1ST ACTOR: Of course. Don't you have anything for me?
3RD ACTOR: Not for you, and not for the Secretary of State either!
1ST ACTOR: Aha! Don't you have anything for me?
3RD ACTOR: NO!
1ST ACTOR: A lathe-operator...
3RD ACTOR: NO!
1ST ACTOR: A mechanic...
3RD ACTOR: NO!
1ST ACTOR: S...
3RD ACTOR: N...
1ST ACTOR: R...
3RD ACTOR: N...
1ST ACTOR: F...
3RD ACTOR: N...

THE STORY OF THE MAN WHO TURNED INTO A DOG

1ST ACTOR: A night-watchman! A night-watchman! Even if it's only a night-watchman!

ACTRESS *(As though playing a trumpet)*: Toot-toot! Toot-toot-toot! The boss!

Actors 2 and 3 signal to each other.

3RD ACTOR *(To the audience)*: The night-watchman's dog, ladies and gentlemen, had died the night before, after twenty-five years of loyal service.

2ND ACTOR: It was a very old dog.

ACTRESS: That's right.

2ND ACTOR *(To the 1st Actor)*: Do you know how to bark?

1ST ACTOR: A lathe-operator...

2ND ACTOR: Do you know how to bark?

1ST ACTOR: A mechanic...

2ND ACTOR: Do you know how to bark?

1ST ACTOR: A brick-layer...

2ND AND 3RD ACTORS: **NO HELP WANTED!**

1ST ACTOR *(Pauses)*: Bow-wow... bow-wow!...

2ND ACTOR: Very good. Congratulations...

3RD ACTOR: Your salary will be one dollar a day, plus room and board.

2ND ACTOR: As you can see, he was earning one dollar more than the real dog.

ACTRESS: When he came home he told me about the job he'd gotten. He was drunk.

1ST ACTOR *(To his wife)*: But they told me that as soon as one of the workers retired, or died, or was fired, they'd give me his job. Hooray, Maria, hooray! Bow-wow... bow-wow!... Hooray, Maria, hooray!

2ND AND 3RD ACTORS: Bow-wow... Hooray, Maria, hooray!

ACTRESS: He was drunk, poor fellow...

1ST ACTOR: And the following night I started to work. *(He squats down on all fours.)*

2ND ACTOR: Is the doghouse too small for you?

1ST ACTOR: I can't squeeze down low enough.

3RD ACTOR: Does it cramp you here?

1ST ACTOR: Yes.

3RD ACTOR: All right, but look: Don't say "yes" to me. You have to start getting into the habit. Say: "Bow-wow... bow-wow!"

2ND ACTOR: Does it cramp you here? *(The 1st Actor does not answer.)* Does it cramp you here?

1ST ACTOR: Bow-wow... bow-wow!...

2ND ACTOR: All right... *(He leaves.)*

1ST ACTOR: But that night it rained, and I had to get into the doghouse.

2ND ACTOR *(To the 3rd Actor):* Now it doesn't cramp him...

3RD ACTOR: And he's in the doghouse.

2ND ACTOR *(To the 1st Actor):* You see how a person can get used to anything?

ACTRESS: A person can get used to anything...

2ND AND 3RD ACTORS: That's right

ACTRESS: And he began to get used to it.

3RD ACTOR: Then, when you see someone coming, you bark: "Bow-wow... bow-wow!" Try it, and let's see...

1ST ACTOR *(As the 2nd Actor comes running up):* Bow-wow..., bow-wow! *(The 2nd Actor approaches cautiously.)* Bow-wow..., bow-wow! *(The 2nd Actor comes slinking up.)* Bow-wow..., bow-wow... bow-wow!... *(He leaves.)*

3RD ACTOR: It will cost us a dollar a day more to do it this way...

2ND ACTOR: Hmmm!

3RD ACTOR: ...but the poor fellow works so hard at it that he deserves the money...

2ND ACTOR: Hmmm!

3RD ACTOR: Besides, he doesn't eat any more than the dead one ate...

2ND ACTOR: Hmmm!

3RD ACTOR: We have to help out his family!

2ND ACTOR: Hmmm! Hmmm! Hmmm! *(He leaves.)*

ACTRESS: And yet, he was always so sad when I saw him. I would try to console him when he came home. *(1st Actor enters.)* We had company today!...

1ST ACTOR: Oh?

ACTRESS: Do you remember the dances we used to go to at the club?

1ST ACTOR: Yes.

ACTRESS: What was our favorite song?

1ST ACTOR: I don't know.

ACTRESS: What do you mean, you don't?! (Sings.) "Gertie got me against the wall..." *(The 1st Actor is down on all fours.)* And one day

THE STORY OF THE MAN WHO TURNED INTO A DOG

you brought me a carnation... *(She looks at him, and draws back, horrified.)* What are you doing?

1ST ACTOR: What?

ACTRESS: You're down on your hands and knees. *(She leaves.)*

1ST ACTOR: I won't take this anymore. I'm going to talk to the boss!

2nd and 3rd Actors enter.

3RD ACTOR: There simply isn't anything else...

1ST ACTOR: Someone told me that an old man just died.

3RD ACTOR: Yes, but we're in an economic pinch at the moment. Wait a little longer, all right?

ACTRESS: And he waited. He went back after three months.

1ST ACTOR: *(To the 2nd Actor.)* They tell me that someone retired...

2ND ACTOR: Yes, but we're going to close that section. Wait just a little while longer, all right?

ACTRESS: And he waited. He went back two months later.

1ST ACTOR: *(To the 3rd Actor.)* Give me the job of one of the men who were fired because they went on strike...

3RD ACTOR: That's impossible. We're not going to fill their jobs...

2ND AND 3RD ACTORS: To set an example! *(They leave.)*

1ST ACTOR: Then I couldn't stand it anymore... and I quit!

ACTRESS: It was the happiest night we'd spent in a long time. *(She takes him by the hand.)* What's the name of this flower?

1ST ACTOR: Flower...

ACTRESS: And what's the name of that star?

1ST ACTOR: Maria.

ACTRESS *(Laughing)*: Maria is my name!

1ST ACTOR: And that's its name too... that's its name too! *(He takes her hand and kisses it.)*

ACTRESS *(Pulling back her hand)*: Don't bite me!

1ST ACTOR I wasn't going to bite you... I was going to kiss you, Maria

ACTRESS: Oh!... I thought you were going to bite me... *(She leaves.)*

2nd and 3rd Actors enter.

2ND ACTOR: Of course...

3RD ACTOR: ...the next morning...

2ND AND 3RD ACTORS: He had to look for another job.

1ST ACTOR: I tried everywhere, until, one place...

3RD ACTOR: Look... We don't have anything for you. Except...

1ST ACTOR: What?

OSVALDO DRAGÚN

3RD ACTOR: Last night the night-watchman's dog died.
2ND ACTOR: He was thirty-five years old, the poor thing...
2ND AND 3RD ACTORS: Poor thing!
1ST ACTOR: And I had to accept again.
2ND ACTOR: Yes, and we paid him one dollar and fifty cents a day. *(2nd and 3rd Actors spin around.)* Hmm!... Hmmm!... Hmmm!...
2ND AND 3RD ACTORS: It's a deal! A dollar and fifty cents! *(They leave.)*
ACTRESS *(Enters):* Of course, forty-five dollars isn't enough to pay our rent.
1ST ACTOR: Look, I have a doghouse. Why don't you move into an apartment with four or five other girls?
ACTRESS: That's the only thing we can do. But we don't have enough to buy food either...
1ST ACTOR: Look, I've gotten used to bones, so I'll bring the meat to you, okay?
2ND AND 3RD ACTORS *(Entering):* The management accepted!
1ST ACTOR AND ACTRESS: The management accepted... Thank goodness! *(2nd and 3rd Actors leave.)*
1ST ACTOR: I was used to it by now. The doghouse seemed larger to me. Walking on all fours wasn't so very different from walking on two feet. Maria and I would meet in the park... *(He goes up to her.)* Because you can't come into my doghouse; and I can't go to your apartment... Until, one night...
ACTRESS: We were taking a walk. And suddenly I felt sick...
1ST ACTOR: What's wrong?
ACTRESS: I feel dizzy.
1ST ACTOR: Why?
ACTRESS *(Weeping):* I think... I'm going to have a baby...
1ST ACTOR: And you're crying because of that?
ACTRESS: I'm afraid... I'm afraid!
1ST ACTOR: But, why?
ACTRESS: I'm afraid... I'm afraid! I don't want to have a baby!
1ST ACTOR: Why, Maria? Why?
ACTRESS: I'm afraid... that it will be a... *(She whispers "dog." The 1st Actor looks at her, horrified, and runs away, barking. He falls to the ground. He stands up.)* He ran off..., he ran away. Sometimes he would stop, and then he would run around on all fours...
1ST ACTOR: That's not true: I didn't stop! I couldn't stop! My back

THE STORY OF THE MAN WHO TURNED INTO A DOG

hurt when I stopped! Bow-wow!... Cars almost ran over me... People would stop and stare... *(2nd and 3rd Actors enter.)* Go away! Haven't you ever seen a dog before?

2ND ACTOR: He's mad! Call a doctor. *(He leaves.)*

3RD ACTOR: He's drunk! Call the police! *(He leaves.)*

ACTRESS: Later they told me that a man felt sorry for him and went up to him affectionately.

2ND ACTOR *(Enters)*: Don't you feel good, buddy? You can't stay down on your hands and knees like that. Do you know how many beautiful things there are to see if you're on your feet, looking up? Stand up... I'll help you... Come on, stand up...

1ST ACTOR *(He begins to stand up, and suddenly)*: Bow-wow..., bow-wow!... *(He bites the man.)* Bow-wow... bow-wow!... *(He leaves.)*

3RD ACTOR *(Enters)*: So, after not seeing him for two years, we asked his wife, "How is he?" And she answered...

ACTRESS: I don't know.

2ND ACTOR: Is he all right?

ACTRESS: I don't know.

3RD ACTOR: Is he sick?

ACTRESS: I don't know.

2ND AND 3RD ACTORS: Where is he?

ACTRESS: In the doghouse.

3RD ACTOR: And when we came here, a prize-fighter passed by...

2ND ACTOR: And they told us that he didn't know how to read, but that that didn't matter because he was a prize-fighter.

3RD ACTOR: And a soldier came by...

ACTRESS: And a policeman came by...

2ND ACTOR: And they came by..., and they came by..., and you came by. And we thought you might be interested in the story of our friend...

ACTRESS: Because there might be a woman out there among you who is thinking right now: "Will I have a..., will I have a...? *(She whispers: "dog.")*

3RD ACTOR: Or there might be a man out there who has been offered a job as a night-watchman's dog.

ACTRESS: If there isn't, we're glad.

2ND ACTOR: But if there is, if one of you is a man they're trying to turn into a dog, like our friend, then... But, well, that... that's

OSVALDO DRAGÚN

another story!

CURTAIN

THE STORY OF PANCHITO GONZÁLEZ

(Who Felt Responsible for the Outbreak of Bubonic Plague in South Africa)

OSVALDO DRAGÚN

OSVALDO DRAGÚN

Actress
Actor 1
Actor 2
Panchito

ACTRESS: This is the story of how our friend Pancho...
ACTOR 1: Panchito.
ACTRESS: Yes, Panchito González, felt responsible for the outbreak of bubonic plague in South Africa.
ACTOR 1: We hadn't seen Panchito for many years; but yesterday when we were strolling around, as usual, collecting stories...
ACTOR 2 *(Going by)*: Extra!... Extra!... Tremendous outbreak of bubonic plague in South Africa!
ACTOR 1: Bubonic plague!...
ACTOR 2 *(Going past again)*: Bubonic plague in South Africa! Extra!...
ACTRESS: South Africa?
ACTOR 1: It's not Brazil...
ACTRESS: It isn't Uruguay...
ACTOR 1: It's a long way from here. There's no danger of it spreading.
ACTRESS: So we went on, but suddenly...
PANCHITO *(Enters and speaks with a gloomy voice)*: Hello.
ACTRESS & ACTOR 1: Panchito! How's it going, old buddy? It's been a long time!...
ACTRESS: Let's go have a cup of coffee! Coffee...
ACTOR 1: Coffee!
PANCHITO: Alka Seltzer.
ACTOR 2 *(Going past)*: Extra! Extra! Outbreak of bubonic plague in South Africa!...
PANCHITO: Come on! Those newspaper boys make me feel awful.
ACTRESS: But Panchito! What's wrong? Been working too hard?
PANCHITO: No.
ACTRESS: In debt?
PANCHITO: No.

THE STORY OF PANCHITO GONZÁLEZ

ACTRESS: Sick?

PANCHITO: Yes. Bubonic plague!

ACTRESS & ACTOR 1 *(Jumping up):* You have... bubonic plague?

PANCHITO: No, not me! The bubonic plague in South Africa! It's my fault...

ACTRESS: And he told us his story. At one time you wanted to be an engineer...

PANCHITO: Yes. I always knew that two times two were four.

ACTOR 1: But it didn't turn out that way for you...

PANCHITO: I got married. Waiter, another Alka Seltzer.

ACTRESS & ACTOR I *(Humming the wedding march):* Dum dum de dum!

PANCHITO: Yes. First a baby boy...

ACTRESS & ACTOR 1 *(Not as happily):* Dum dum de dum!

PANCHITO: Then a little girl...

ACTRESS & ACTOR 1 *(Depressed):* Dum dum de dum...

ACTOR 1: And then?

PANCHITO: Twins.

ACTRESS & ACTOR 1 *(Gloomily):* Dum dum de... dum...

PANCHITO: And then I thought to myself: An engineer? Hah! *(Ironic.)* Sure, anytime! And I had to find a job to support my family...

ACTRESS *(Now his wife):* Look, honey, why don't you go talk to my uncle. He works for a congressman...

ACTOR 1: Why, of course, my boy! Take this letter to the Trans-Oceanic Meat Corporation. They owe me a few favors, and they'll hire you... they'll hire you.

ACTOR 2 *(Enters):* Mr. Gun-zaleez!

ACTRESS: One of the owners was English.

ACTOR 1: Signore Gonzalo!

ACTRESS: And the other was Italian. Naturally: it was Trans-Oceanic!

PANCHITO *(To his wife):* They hired me! I make 1,500 pesos a month...

ACTRESS: Wonderful!...

PANCHITO: No! Not so wonderful! What can we do with 1,500 pesos? Eat beans.

ACTRESS: Be patient, Panchito. Wait for opportunity to knock...

PANCHITO: And opportunity knocked.

ACTORS 1 & 2: Ta-ra-ta-ra... ta-ra-ta-ra... Da dat... di, da dat, di, da da dat... Cable for Trans-Oceanic Meat Corporation.

ACTOR 2 *(Reads, pronouncing Spanish words badly):* "We have been granted the honor of bidding to supply two thousand tons of *carnee* to the *pueeblos* of South Africa. It all depends on the price we can offer."

ACTOR 1 *(Heavy Italian accent):* Anything that'sa meaty, it's-a good!...

ACTOR 2 *(Calls):* Mister *Pan*-chito!

ACTOR 1: Signore Gonzalo!

PANCHITO *(To his wife):* They called *me*, honey! Me! To a meeting with the board of directors. I just know they're going to give me a raise.

ACTRESS: Good. But don't get so excited—your tie is all twisted. Whoo! Why do you use that cologne?

PANCHITO: Because it's cheap. Besides, it's called "Beso de amor"— Kiss of love. See? *(He kisses her.)*

ACTRESS: Hush up, you nut. And call me as soon as you find out something.

PANCHITO: So I went to the meeting of the board of directors...

ACTOR 2: Mister *Pan*-chito. That is the question. *Carnee*, or not *carnee*...

ACTOR 1: We've gotta be cheaper than all-a the rest-a.

ACTOR 2: It all depends on *yoo-stéd*. We'll give you 5,000 *pay-soos* a month if you solve our problem...

PANCHITO *(On the telephone):* Hello!... Hello, hello!...

ACTRESS: Hello!

PANCHITO: Honey, I got it! 5,000 pesos a month!

ACTRESS: Darling! I'll bake a cake to celebrate.

PANCHITO: Sure. The cake was fine, but the competition was terrible...

ACTOR 1: Four pesos for a kilo of beef!

ACTOR 2: Three pesos for a kilo of mutton!

ACTOR 1: Two pesos for a kilo of pork!

ACTOR 2: One-fifty for a kilo of tripe!

PANCHITO: It was terrible! I couldn't compete...

ACTOR 2: Mister *Pan*-chito, about your 5,000 pay-soos... *(He shakes his head.)*

ACTOR 1: Eh!... This is-a bad... It's-a bad-a, signore Gonzalo...

PANCHITO: And me, what could I do? It was 5,000 pesos a month, and I had to support my family. Think, Panchito, think... That's it! *(To Actors 2 & 3):* Ask them! Please ask them! It's the only way!

ACTOR 2: Hello, London. Urgent!

ACTOR 1: Roma, presto!

THE STORY OF PANCHITO GONZÁLEZ

PANCHITO: I had to wait two days for the answer. Two days! And every time I saw one of the kids eating, or riding the bike I bought them, I got scared. What if we'd have to go back to eating beans?

ACTORS 1 & 2: Ta-ta-ra-ta-ra… Ta-ta-ra-ta-ra… Cable for the Trans-Oceanic Meat Corporation!

PANCHITO: Finally the answer arrived! Yes?...

ACTOR 2: Mister *Pan*-chito, it needn't be beef…

ACTOR 1: Anything's okay, so long as it's-a meat! Besides…, the Africans—they're all-a black…

PANCHITO: They were black, you understand? They aren't like us. They… they're black, see?

ACTOR 2: And also, they tell us the label should be in several colors. The Nigras like colors.

PANCHITO: You see? The kind of meat didn't matter. It was the label… the damned colors… And for me it meant 5,000 pesos! What else could I do? So I did it. *(He whispers in the ear of Actor 1.)*

ACTOR 1: But-a no, signore Gonzalo! In Italia i poveri mangianno anche horsemeat. It's-a bonna meat!

PANCHITO: Horsemeat wouldn't work because the poor people in Italy eat it. *(He whispers in the ear of Actor 2.)*

ACTOR 2: Noo, noo, Mister *Pan*-chito. Dog meat with *vee-noo blank-oo* is very *bien*, very *bien*!

PANCHITO: Dog meat wouldn't work because the lords of London eat it. And for me it meant 5,000 pesos! What could I do? Think, Panchito, think! Think… That's it! No, no, not that… not that… no… Well, all right! Rat-meat!

ACTORS 1 & 2: Rat-meat? Ugh!

PANCHITO: But they accepted, and we got the contract.

ACTOR 1: Bravo, bravo, signore Gonzalo!

ACTOR 2: Mister *Pan*-chito, the 5,000 *pay-soos* are yours!

PANCHITO: So I went home, and asked my wife to bake another cake. *(To the Actress):* Where are the children?

ACTRESS: In bed.

PANCHITO: Didn't you bake a cake?

ACTRESS: No, I didn't.

PANCHITO: Why not?

ACTRESS: Look, I don't like the way you've been acting lately. You've changed.

PANCHITO: How did I use to be?

OSVALDO DRAGÚN

ACTRESS: You cared about other people.

PANCHITO: I still do! But these Negroes... They're not people...

ACTRESS: What do *you* know?

PANCHITO: I know! Besides, it means 5,000 pesos. And if we hadn't gotten married, I'd be an engineer now. But since I married you and I'm not an engineer, I have to scratch for a living... *(The Actress goes out.)* She left. I hurt her feelings. All this trouble for a bunch of African Niggers! But my conscience bothered me... So the next day... *(To Actor 2):* Tell me, Doctor, do you think rat meat could hurt Negroes?

ACTOR 2: Absolutely not. Rat meat is what cats eat. Cats live in people's houses. Men eat beef. So it's the same for a Negro to eat rat meat as for him to eat beef. I'm going, m'boy. There's a nice barbecued steak waiting for me in my chalet in the country... *(He leaves.)*

PANCHITO: You see? They were Negroes! But, still, I went to see a lawyer. *(To Actor 1):* Is it legal or not?

ACTOR 1 There is no jurisprudence,

on this sort of incident,

nor to my knowledge

is there legal precedent...

PANCHITO: But is it legal or not?

ACTOR 1: How the heck should I know?

PANCHITO: So I went to see a scientist... *(To Actor 2):* What is your opinion, Professor?

ACTOR 2: Now, you see, the Negroes are an inferior race who live in a primitive animal state. They eat each other, which means that they eat animals. So that to eat a tiny rat would only mean that they would be eating a smaller type of animal. Pardon me, but I really must go... I've been invited to a lecture on the origins of Sanskrit.

PANCHITO: And then I made up my mind. *(He announces very loudly):*

The Trans-Oceanic Meat Corporation is about to undertake its great campaign of deratization!

ACTOR 1 *(Calling):* Here rat, here rat, here rat...

ACTOR 2: Here, rattie, rattie, rattie...

ACTOR 1: Rat, rattie... rat, rattie...

ACTOR 2: A hundred rats!

ACTOR 1: A thousand rats!

PANCHITO: Four million rats!

THE STORY OF PANCHITO GONZÁLEZ

ACTRESS: At that time I hardly ever saw him. He was very busy! And I had time to think. And I thought that maybe it was all my fault that he had children, and hadn't been able to become an engineer. Now he was turning into a big businessman. And anything he didn't like he'd call "Nigger."

ACTOR 1: Mr. González, Fernández called to say he would be late…

PANCHITO: Fire that damn Nigger!

ACTOR 2: Isn't it hot, Mr. González!

PANCHITO: It's because of that damn nigger of a sun.

ACTRESS: You got your clothes all dirty!

PANCHITO: A nigger of a car splashed that damn nigger mud on me.

ACTRESS: And he read books about the Ku-Klux-Klan… He was trying to convince himself. Until one day City Hall called him. I had to go with him…

ACTOR 2: Our fair city is honored to be able to present to you the Distinguished Cross of Public Health on behalf of the service rendered by you through your great campaign against rats… Ladies and gentlemen, a toast to the new Pied-Piper of… of… *(Actor 1 whispers in his ear).* Oh, yes! Of that, of that.

ACTRESS: I left before it was over. I didn't like it at all…

PANCHITO: Now we have to think about the colored labels!

ACTOR 1: Signore Gonzalo, the colors, they should-a be blue, yellow and-a blue…

ACTOR 2: Noo, noo! I propose a contest for painters. To the winner, 10,000 *pay-soos* and a scholarship to London. It will be… artistical.

PANCHITO: And we made it artistic. The painters of concretism came.

ACTOR 1: I suggest a tree that becomes a ham sandwich…

PANCHITO: What color?

ACTOR 1: Red and white, of course!

PANCHITO: No good. The abstract painters came…

ACTOR 2: I have in mind a cube traversed by a series of dots that…

PANCHITO: What color?

ACTOR 2: Green and black!

PANCHITO: No good.

ACTOR 2: Well!… *(He leaves.)*

PANCHITO: And finally a surrealist woman…

ACTRESS: I suggest the eye of Hamlet's ghost, pierced by the toothpick that his uncle used during the celebration…

OSVALDO DRAGÚN

PANCHITO: What color?

ACTRESS: Red, yellow, violet, orange, green, black…

PANCHITO: Perfect! We made the labels with the eye and the toothpick, the surrealist went to London, and the meat went to Africa. A week passed…

ACTOR 1 *(To Actor 2):* Captain, don't you smell something strange?

ACTOR 2: It's the smell of the ocean…

PANCHITO: Another week passed...

ACTOR 1: Captain, something stinks!

ACTOR 2: It's the sea air.

PANCHITO: And the following week…

ACTOR 1 *(Holding his nose, nearly fainting):* Will it take much longer, Captain?

ACTOR 2: No, we'll be there tomorrow.

ACTOR 1: I can't stand the smell!

ACTOR 2: It's the crap in those cans that we're carrying below! It smells worse than dead rats!

PANCHITO: But it *was* dead rats! And how could I be to blame if the doctor, the lawyer and the professor all told me that it didn't matter. And how could I be to blame if I had to support my family, and 5,000 pesos is 5,000 pesos. Besides, they were Negroes… and nothing could happen to them. Isn't that right?—that nothing could happen to them?

ACTOR 1 *(Offers something to Actor 2):* Pretty color, huh? Pretty color!

ACTOR 2 *(Transformed into an African Negro):* Pretty color! Pretty color! *(He opens the can, eats, his eyes spin, and he falls down dead, his feet and hands rigid, like a dog.)*

ACTOR 1: Extra!... Extra!... Outbreak of bubonic plague in South Africa! Bubonic plague! Bubonic plague in South Africa!...

ACTOR 2: Mister *Pan*-chito.

ACTOR 1: Signore Gonzalo, your idea, it's-a not-a so good.

ACTOR 2: Mister *Pan*-chito, *yoo-stéd* are not hoo-manitarian, and our company must be hoo-manitarian, you know? *(They shake hands with him and leave.)*

PANCHITO: And they fired me. Can you believe it? Of course, it was probably all my fault. Bubonic plague! You know? The poor Negroes!

ACTOR 2 *(Passing by):* Outbreak of bubonic plague in South Africa! Outbreak of bubonic plague in South Africa!... *(He leaves.)*

THE STORY OF PANCHITO GONZÁLEZ

PANCHITO: Stop it, please! Do you want me to throw myself in the river?

ACTOR 1: This was the story that Panchito told us…

ACTRESS *(Laughing):* And he really made us laugh!

PANCHITO: No, please, don't laugh! Don't laugh! It's very serious!

ACTRESS: But, Panchito…

PANCHITO: It's very serious, I tell you! Because now I feel sorry for the Negroes in South Africa. But what if tomorrow they offer me 5,000 pesos to do the very same thing? What will I do? I have to think about my family, and 5,000 pesos is 5,000 pesos! And what if instead of the Africans it's the people who live here. What will I do? I swear that I don't know. And that makes me stop and think. Besides, my wife told me that I wasn't the same anymore. That I'd changed. And that makes me stop and think too. Don't laugh, please. Don't laugh!…

ACTOR 1: And of course…

ACTRESS: Then… we didn't laugh anymore.

CURTAIN

R.I.P.

JOSÉ MARTÍNEZ QUEIROLO

JOSÉ MARTÍNEZ QUIEROLO

JOSÉ MARTÍNEZ QUEIROLO

Ecuador: 1931-2008

José Martínez Quieirolo (or "Pipo," as he was known to his friends) was a writer of short stories and dramas, many of which offer a critique and parody of Ecuadoran society. First studying to be a civil engineer, he left school to devote his time to writing. He began to appear prominently in theatrical circles not long after the advent of other Ecuadoran literary giants who also wrote for the theatre, such as Demetrio Aguilera Malta and Jorge Icaza.

Winning several awards in his home country, his plays have been translated into other languages and have been presented on stages in Europe and the U.S.A. Invited to Russia and to the United States, he nonetheless opted to remain in Ecuador and practice his artistry there.

The play, *R.I.P.* was first performed in Guayaquil, Ecuador in 1969 by the group "Los Guayacanes," of which he was director. It offers a biting satire of a certain social class of that country.

R. I. P.

The Author: José Martínez Queirolo
The Director: Miguel Sarracín

The Actors: Isabel Martínez and Antonio Santos and the other
members of the Grupo Guayacanes have the profound satisfaction
of informing you
of the tragic death of
Simon Rhubarb and his wife, Henrietta Rhubarb
(R.I.P.)
and invite you to the bearing of their mortal remains from the Casa de la
Cultura, Guayas branch, to the main Cemetery, tonight at 9:30 p.m.
Your attendance will leave them eternally grateful.

Guayaquil, July 1969.

CHARACTERS:

Henrietta
Simon

A voice. The sound of religious hymns and prayers. Two chairs on a starkly lighted stage. Sitting there, their eyes closed, their hands crossed over their chests, are Henrietta and Simon. A long pause.

HENRIETTA: Simon, are you there?
SIMON: Yes, I'm here!... What about you?
HENRIETTA: I'm here too!
They slowly open their eyes.
HENRIETTA: Look at all the people!
SIMON: Henrietta, are your eyes...?
HENRIETTA: They're open, just like yours, Simon. But every once in a while a hand comes up and closes them.

JOSÉ MARTÍNEZ QUIEROLO

SIMON: Every so often my jaw falls open…, my jaw falls open and somebody puts it back in place!
HENRIETTA: How considerate they are! Did you see the wreaths? The chrysanthemums…, carnations…, lilies… That beautiful cross over there on your right.
SIMON: From Count Sanjurjo y Calatrava.
HENRIETTA: Count Sanjurjo…? But he's dead!
SIMON: Well, he sympathizes with us…! *(He continues to read the cards.)* The staff of the Rhubarb Company, the employees of the Rhubarb Company.
HENRIETTA: They're paper flowers.
SIMON: Well, anyway, it's a touching scene.
HENRIETTA: Oh, if only we could feel touched! *(They close their eyes brusquely. A pause.)*
HENRIETTA: Simon! Simon!
SIMON: I'm here, Henrietta!
HENRIETTA: Do you feel anything special?
SIMON: Special…? No, not exactly. Just the cold, as usual.
HENRIETTA: The cold, always the cold. I wish they'd give us some whiskey!
SIMON: At this stage I doubt that even whiskey would revive us!
HENRIETTA: I can't get angry. "It was Simon's fault!... It was Simon's fault!..." That's what I keep thinking, that's what I keep repeating, but nothing works!
SIMON: Let's keep trying, dear. It might work!
HENRIETTA: You were to blame!
SIMON: You were!
HENRIETTA: You! You!
SIMON: You! You! You!
HENRIETTA: You! You! You! You! You!
SIMON: Are you getting excited, dear?
HENRIETTA: I think so! Let's keep it up.
BOTH OF THEM *(Imitating the jerking movements and the growing noise of a car engine starting up):* You! You! You! You! You!
HENRIETTA: Who was driving? You! You! You! You!
SIMON: Who was in a hurry? Faster, you shouted. Faster! Faster! You! You! You! You!
HENRIETTA: We had to get there. It was a benefit ball.
SIMON: For your benefit!

R. I. P.

HENRIETTA: It was for poor children!

SIMON: It was for your vanity!... They were going to pick the best dressed woman in the city, and you were certain that you would win...

HENRIETTA: The best dressed woman in the city!... And aren't I?

SIMON: You *were*, Henrietta!

HENRIETTA: I am! I am! Look at my shroud!

SIMON *(Opening his eyes, then immediately closing them again)*: Huh!

HENRIETTA: I am! I was!... I was certain to win that night! And you were proud too! You! You! You!

SIMON: You! You! You! You!

HENRIETTA: We both were, darling! Both of us!... We were so happy!

SIMON: Drunk, you mean!

HENRIETTA: Happy and in a hurry!... We had to get there!

SIMON: Yes, and you see what happened... We didn't get there!

HENRIETTA: Suddenly that man was there, waving at us!

SIMON: Standing right in the middle of the road, waving at us!

HENRIETTA: He wanted us to pick him up!

SIMON: No, no. He wanted to warn us about that tree that had fallen down...

HENRIETTA: Don't stop! Keep going!

SIMON: That's exactly what you said!... And I kept going!... I kept going!

BOTH OF THEM *(Opening their eyes wide)*: THUD! BANG! CRAAASH!

HENRIETTA: You idiot! You absolute idiot!

SIMON: Darling. Are you getting excited?

HENRIETTA: I'm trying, but it's not working! *(They close their eyes. A pause.)*

SIMON: Let's think about the victim. A poor, defenseless man.

HENRIETTA: But was there only *one* victim?... There were two! The two of us!

SIMON: No, Henrietta, dear. Look at us, we're still the same. But the man, that man, he was so full of life!

HENRIETTA: Faster! Faster!

SIMON: Such a poor fellow; probably a farmer.

HENRIETTA: Faster! Faster!

SIMON: A nice, respectable farmer. A family man.

JOSÉ MARTÍNEZ QUIEROLO

HENRIETTA: A family man…, a family man…
SIMON: You're getting flushed, dear!
HENRIETTA: On the contrary, I'm getting cold.
SIMON: Let's accept our guilt; maybe it will work that way!… I was to blame!
HENRIETTA: I was!
SIMON: Me! Me!
HENRIETTA: Me! Me! Me!
SIMON: Me! Me! Me! Me! Me!
HENRIETTA: It's no good, Simon. We don't have a conscience!
SIMON: No, we never did. It's still cold.
HENRIETTA: The cold, still the same cold… *(A pause. They slowly open their eyes.)*
HENRIETTA: People are still coming!
SIMON: It's nearly time, our time.
HENRIETTA: How popular we are! Look how much they love us!
SIMON: Yes, but nobody is crying!
HENRIETTA: That's true, no one is crying… Simon, how do I look?
SIMON: Very pale, very pale… There's a green fly on your nose!
HENRIETTA: Oh! *(Grimacing.)* Shoo it away!… Shoo the fly away!
SIMON: Isn't there a gentleman here who will brush the fly away from my wife?
HENRIETTA: The fly!… The fly!… My kingdom for a flyswatter! *(To the gentleman.)* Thank you very much; so kind of you!… *(They both close their eyes. To Simon.)* Who is he? I don't remember him.
SIMON: Johnny Dung.
HENRIETTA: What a nice young man. Does he come from a good family?
SIMON: They don't have any money. He goes to all the better funerals, so that he can hob nob with high society.
HENRIETTA: I'll remember that! Now, how do I look?
SIMON *(Opening his eyes)*: More pale than ever, and very thin.
HENRIETTA: Don't I look any younger?
SIMON: You're as old as you are. You look like a ghost!
HENRIETTA: In the United States they would have fixed me up, but here…, how negligent they are!
SIMON: Well, you know, Henrietta, it's an "underdeveloped" country!
HENRIETTA *(Opening her eyes)*: To die, to die over there!… How beautiful that would have been!… And to come back as an imported

R. I. P.

corpse!... Simon, it's on you now!

SIMON: What?

HENRIETTA: The fly!

SIMON *(Screwing up his face):* The fly!... The fly!

HENRIETTA: Watch out for your mouth!... *(Simon continues wriggling his face with his mouth closed.)* Johnny Dung! Shoo the fly away from my husband!... *(To Simon.)* Calm down; it flew away! *(Pause.)*

HENRIETTA: The time is getting closer, and the children haven't come yet.

SIMON: They won't come. Europe is a long way from here.

HENRIETTA: They probably didn't have time to catch the plane.

SIMON: No. They never have time for anything!

HENRIETTA: Time to write!

SIMON: Time to study!

HENRIETTA: They don't know, Simon. No one has told them!

SIMON: They'll find out at the end of the month!

HENRIETTA: Yes. At the end of the month they'll miss us!

SIMON: Us, or the check?

HENRIETTA: Us, Simon... when the check doesn't come!

SIMON: Orphans and fools... What a couple of beneficiaries we're leaving behind!

HENRIETTA: What will become of our money?

SIMON: Our bank accounts! Our property!

HENRIETTA: The furniture, the estate!...

SIMON: The interest, the stocks, the investments!...

HENRIETTA: Look how Gonzalez's eyes are shining!

SIMON: Look how Rodriguez's hands are trembling!

HENRIETTA: It's almost time. Let's try once more!

SIMON: What can we do?

HENRIETTA: Maybe if we fight!... Call me a bitch!

SIMON: Bitch! Bitch! Bitch!

HENRIETTA: Are you yawning?

SIMON: No, I'm sighing! Bitch!

HENRIETTA: You bastard!

SIMON: Nothing?

HENRIETTA: Nothing!... Do you remember the first time?

SIMON: Act one, scene one, of our Conjugal Life.

HENRIETTA: That was heaven! I almost loved you then!... Later the insults began to lose their effect.

SIMON: The insults or the truth?
HENRIETTA: The truth... And then, I couldn't anymore.
SIMON: They wouldn't let you. Every one of your lovers was jealous!
HENRIETTA: Yours were too! But now, now... Do you know what?
SIMON: What?
HENRIETTA: My breasts, Simon!
SIMON: What about your breasts?
HENRIETTA: They're getting firm!
SIMON: Ah!
HENRIETTA: Oh!
SIMON: Ah!
HENRIETTA: Doesn't that excite you, dear?
SIMON: Dear, I'm so cold
HENRIETTA: R. I. P.!
SIMON: R. I. P.?
HENRIETTA: Simon! Maybe we should get a separation... A separation of bodies and property. Isn't there such a thing as a divorce in extremis?
SIMON: No. Not an in extremis divorce, or even a post-mortem one!
HENRIETTA: So, we'll be together?
SIMON: Together!... Uselessly together for all Eternity! *(A pause. The sound of religious hymns and prayers.)*
HENRIETTA: Simon! It's raining!
SIMON: That's the holy water. They're exorcizing us, dearest!
HENRIETTA: Do you suppose it's really true that there's a heaven?
SIMON: Well, if there's a heaven... there's a hell!
HENRIETTA: Ah!
SIMON: Oh!
HENRIETTA: Ah!... Look how Fernandez's eyes are shining!
SIMON: Look how Raimundo's hands are trembling!
HENRIETTA: Raimundo's and everyone else's!
SIMON: They're coming closer!
HENRIETTA: Yes, they're coming closer!
SIMON: They smell fresh money. The vultures!
HENRIETTA: Vultures!... Shoo!
SIMON: Shoo!
HENRIETTA: Scat!

The light goes out with a dull thud. Henrietta and Simon remain seated with their eyes open, and a light shining on their faces. From this point on they can move

R. I. P.

as the coffin they are supposedly in moves.

HENRIETTA: Did you see that, Simon?

SIMON: They closed the lid on us!

HENRIETTA: It's not time yet. It isn't five-thirty!

BOTH OF THEM: Open up!... Open up!

SIMON: Can you feel them lifting us?

HENRIETTA: They're tilting me.

SIMON: It's the stairs. They're taking us down now.

HENRIETTA: Be careful!... Don't bump into anything!...

SIMON: The street, the hearse... A first class burial.

HENRIETTA: The chauffeur driving the hearse is terribly reckless!... Why is he going so fast?

SIMON: He probably has another appointment.

HENRIETTA *(To the Chauffeur):* Slow down. Not so fast!... Be careful!

SIMON: We're there... Now they're taking us out. They're carrying us on their shoulders to our new mansion.

HENRIETTA: Now what's happening! Why are we stopping?

SIMON: The photographers!... Smile! *(They smile.)*

HENRIETTA: Who's carrying my coffin?

SIMON: I'm not sure! I don't know them.

HENRIETTA: What about the attendants?... Who are the attendants?

SIMON: The Governor...

HENRIETTA: The Mayor...

SIMON: The Chancellor of the University...

HENRIETTA: Newspaper editors, and Ministers...

SIMON: Didn't the President come?

HENRIETTA: I don't know! I can't see him anywhere!... What about the Archbishop? I don't see the Archbishop!

SIMON: He's in the first row!

HENRIETTA: He's always so considerate.

SIMON: The civil authorities, the military and the church officials.

HENRIETTA: From left to right, as they'll say in the newspapers tomorrow.

SIMON: That's right!...

HENRIETTA: How popular we are! Look at all the people here!

SIMON: Church officials, the oligarchy...

HENRIETTA: Bureaucrats, politicians, financiers...

SIMON: Bankers, businessmen, smugglers...

HENRIETTA: Smugglers, merchants, speculators!

JOSÉ MARTÍNEZ QUIEROLO

SIMON: Gentlemen and ladies!
HENRIETTA *(Correcting him):* Ladies and gentlemen!
SIMON: Happy women…
HENRIETTA: Sad women...
SIMON: Happily sad women… Bitches, bitch!
HENRIETTA: Bastards, bastard!
SIMON: Decent people, indecent people…
HENRIETTA: Go-go!
SIMON: Ye-ye!
HENRIETTA: Homos, perverts, pimps… A little bit of everything, Simon!
SIMON: And of that little bit, the best!
HENRIETTA: And there, in back, in the rear.
SIMON: The staff and employees of Rhubarb & Co.
HENRIETTA: It's really touching!
SIMON: Ah, if only we could feel touched!
HENRIETTA: Simon!
SIMON: Henrietta!
HENRIETTA: The Secretary of the Syndicate!… The communist!
SIMON: Where?
FIENRIETTA: Over there!… In back of Count Sanjurjo's mausoleum.
SIMON: It is him!… You're right.
HENRIETTA: He came too!… You see, way down deep, he really liked us.
SIMON: Don't you believe it, Henrietta!
HENRIETTA: You think?…
SIMON: He has something up his sleeve, you can count on it. He's probably here to pass out leaflets!
HENRIETTA: Ah!
SIMON: Oh!
HENRIETTA: Ah!
A VOICE: Simon Rhubarb! Henrietta Rhubarb!… In the name of a society deprived of two of its most distinguished and beloved members… in the name of the *dolce vita* that you have left for the *dolce morte*…, my heart heavy with pain, I come before you to deliver the eulogy *de rigueur*.
SIMON: That's Raimundo's voice!
HENRIETTA: The old hypocrite!
VOICE: Knowing as we do of your frequent trips around the world, it

R. I. P.

would not seem at all strange if—when your journey was finished in this Valley of Tears—you decided to embark on Charon's yacht, to undertake a pleasure trip to the other world. Nevertheless, this, being as it is, a matter of a one way voyage, we do not want to believe that so suddenly—without a farewell party, with no luggage—you have already embarked... *(Crying.)* Henrietta! Simon! Dear friends!... Have you truly gone?

BOTH OF THEM: Here we are! Here we are!

VOICE: Your silence is eloquent, and only confirms, once more, what we do not wish to believe... Why go on then? Why continue wasting useless words, when you have decided to leave us forever?

BOTH OF THEM: Wait! Wait!

VOICE: "The dead man to his hole and the live one to his bowl," as the saying goes. So, dear friends, united forever in death as in life. Rest in peace!... Henrietta and Simon!... Farewell!... Farewell!... *(He goes off.)*

HENRIETTA: They're leaving us!

SIMON: They're going away!

HENRIETTA: Goodbye, Raimundo! Goodbye, everybody!

SIMON *(Correcting her):* You mean, "See you soon," Henrietta!

HENRIETTA: That's right! See you soon!... See you soon!... *(A long pause.)*

HENRIETTA: Simon, are you there?

SIMON: I'm here!... What about you?

HENRIETTA: I'm here too!

HENRIETTA: Alone, at last!

SIMON: At last.

HENRIETTA: A beautiful mausoleum!

SIMON: Right in the suburbs, across from Sanjurjo's tomb...

HENRIETTA: With a bar and central heating?

SIMON: Of course!

HENRIETTA: But no one has come out to meet us, to welcome us. What bad manners, Simon!

SIMON: A slight oversight! ... *(Calling out, with a child's voice.)* Daddy!... Mommy!... Your little "Simey" is here... *(A pause.)* Grandpa!... Grandma!... Simey got married, and now he's bringing your new granddaughter for you to meet.

HENRIETTA: My name is Henrietta, Daddy and Mommy..., and you can call me "Rietta!..." I'm from a wealthy family, and I'm respectable. Simey proved that I was still a virgin before our wedding! *(A pause.)* Mr. Rhubarb & Co.... Are they here?

SIMON *(In a hushed voice)*: Rhubarb I is on the left. Rhubarb II is on the right. Rhubarb III is out in a common grave because he was a bastard. My old man is right on top of you.

HENRIETTA: You first, and then him!... Move over a little, Mr. Rhubarb.

SIMON: I'll bet they're all peeved because I didn't come to visit them last All Souls Day... *(Calling out.)* Hello!... Hark...

HENRIETTA *(Idem)*: Hark...

SIMON: Nothing?

HENRIETTA: No one!

SIMON: They must have gone out to mourn. *(A pause.)* Do you feel anything in particular?

HENRIETTA: No, not exactly. Just the same as usual.

SIMON: We should prepare ourselves for our new life.

HENRIETTA: What difference will there be?

SIMON: Our hair and our fingernails will grow out.

HENRIETTA: I asked Evangeline to come every so often to comb my hair and give me a manicure. As for the rest...

SIMON: Are you getting bored?

HENRIETTA: Yes, I'm bored!

SIMON: We have to do something, anything...

HENRIETTA: Suppose I invite the neighbors and we organize a *danse macabre*.

SIMON: Huh!

HENRIETTA: All right, then!... Let's talk about everybody else's affairs.

SIMON: That subject's been worn out. There's nothing left to say!

HENRIETTA: But, Simon! We have to kill time somehow!

SIMON: It's dead already!... Maybe if you could think of something new, something interesting... something we haven't done yet!

HENRIETTA: How about retracing our steps like other ghosts?

SIMON: Going back to the old lies, pretending, exploiting.

HENRIETTA: Exploiting, robbing, fornicating!

SIMON: Huh!

A pause. The light shining on their faces begins to turn green.

HENRIETTA: Are we starting to stink?

SIMON: As usual, my dear! *(A pause.)* Heh!

R. I. P.

HENRIETTA: What is it?
SIMON: I don't know. Something's tickling me!... Heh! Heh!
HENRIETTA: Hee! Me too!
SIMON: Heh! Heh!
HENRIETTA: Hee! Hee!
SIMON: The worms, dearest!
HENRIETTA: The worms, Simon!
SIMON: They're coming out of my head, heh!
HENRIETTA: They're coming out of my heart, hee!
SIMON: Heh! Heh! Heh!
HENRIETTA: Hee! Hee! Hee!
SIMON: At last!
HENRIETTA: At last!
SIMON: This is really living!
HENRIETTA: It's better than whiskey!
SIMON: Better than drugs!
HENRIETTA: Much, much better!
SIMON: Bite me, you nice little worm!
HENRIETTA: Eat me up, you nice little worm!
SIMON: Yes! Yes! That's it!
HENRIETTA: Hee! Hee! Hee!
SIMON: Heh! Heh! Heh!
They are dying with laughter, as the light grows dim and the stage sinks into darkness.

THE END

ROMEO BEFORE THE CORPSE OF JULIET

By George Cahoon

Adapted by MARCO DENEVI

MARCO DENEVI

MARCO DENEVI

Argentina: 1922-1998

Marco Denevi was an award-winning author of novels, short stories and dramas; he was also a lawyer and a journalist. His mystery novel, *Rosaura a las diez* (translated into English as *Rosa at Ten O'clock*), written in 1955, was a Kraft award winner and became a best-seller. His novel, *Ceremonia secreta* (1960), was translated into English, French, Italian, Japanese and other languages, and in 1968 became a film entitled *Silent Ceremony*, starring Elizabeth Taylor, Mia Farrow, Robert Mitchum and Peggy Ashcroft.

Denevi wrote several successful plays, the best known being, perhaps, *Los expedientes* (Dossiers), *El emperador de la China* (The Emperor of China), and *El cuarto de la noche* (The Room at Night). He also wrote scripts for television, worked as a political journalist for *La nación*, and was inducted into the Argentine Academy of Letters in 1987.

ROMEO BEFORE THE CORPSE OF JULIET

CHARACTERS:

Juliet
Romeo
Pages
Friar Laurence

The crypt of the Capulet's mausoleum in Verona. As the curtain rises we see a funeral pyre in the semidarkness on which lies the corpse of Juliet. Romeo enters with a burning torch. He approaches the pyre. Silently he contemplates the body of his beloved. Then he turns to face the audience.

ROMEO: So, then, it was true! Juliet lies dead, by her own hand! Swift messengers, their tale-bearing faces hidden behind masks of false pain, sped to Mantua to bring me the news. But, together with that news, they made the very air resound with the intimation that I return; the threat that if I did not, they would bear me here by force. Each took his leave of me with the same words of farewell: "Romeo, thou knowest now thy duty." I have understood. I have returned. I am here. I encountered no one on the road. No one crossed my path to impede my arrival at this lugubrious site, my lonely watch of this, the corpse of Juliet. Excessive happenstance, destiny's too-full benevolence, suspicious and suspecting fate. Oh, bawdry of the night, what is your price? Those who have bribed you now spy upon me, lodgers in your shadows. They await your deliverance of that which you have promised them. And what have you promised them, rogue of night? My own death! Thus may they find an end to this story that so offends them, and that in its depths compromises them so fastidiously. Juliet has written half the epilogue. And now it remains for me to add the other half so that the curtain may descend amid tears and applause, and they may rise from their seats, greet one another, reconcile themselves with those who were their enemies: you, Montague, with you, Capulet, and then return to their homes to eat, to sleep, to fornicate, and to go on living. And if I do not do it willingly, then they shall force me against my will. They will call me Romeo the fool, impotent lover, vile coward. All doors will close to me. I shall be dealt with as the worst of offenders.

MARCO DENEVI

They will at last accuse me as the assassin of Juliet, and some one of them will deem himself the rightful avenger of that crime. Either I shall write the ending, or they, but always with this same ink: my blood. Were it not so, the death of Juliet should bring them pangs of guilt. With our deaths Juliet and I exchange our share of blame, and they remain free. *(To Juliet.)* Seest thou not, thou hare-brained maid? Seest thou not what thou hast done? Had'st thou need to oblige me to so much? Of what necessity was it to find recourse in these excesses? We loved, 'tis true, we loved. But beyond that point there was no need to pass. To love has meaning only while one does live. For afterward, what does it matter? Now hast thou entwined me in this sinister game, and I, wish it or no, must go on playing. Thou hast placed me twixt the sword and the wall. Without my own consent, 'tis certain. I was born to love, but to play no hero's part. I am a common man, no maniacal suicide. But thou, with news of thy death on every tongue, hast thyself to an unearthly height exalted to which I too must rise, that I might be no less than thou, that I be worthy of thy love, that I cease not to be Romeo. Oh, wretched paradox! That I might never cease being Romeo must I cease to be Romeo. *(To the audience.)* This do I suffer for loving adolescent maidens. They bear it all too seriously. Their love is a constant extortion. Either the bridal bed or the sepulcher. No word of moderation, of concessions, of restraint, of mutual accord. And doing thusly, do they aid the selfish designs of their elders who avail themselves of that unyielding spirit to break their will like dry timber. *(With another tone.)* But that I will not do. I shall not emulate their error. All this is naught but concealment, drawn with one purpose only: to entrap me. Gentlemen, m'ladies, I will not place my foot in the snare. I love Juliet. I shall love her till my death. I shall weep for her till my tears run dry. But expect not more than that from me. Demand no more. For life will justify our love, while no love is sufficient cause to die. Farewell.

He throws the torch in a corner where it is extinguished. He wraps his cloak around himself and exits. The stage remains empty for a few moments. Then two pages enter, bearing the corpse of Romeo with a dagger in his chest. They lay him at the foot of the funeral pyre. One of the pages places Romeo's hand on the handle of the dagger. They step back. Friar Laurence enters. He kneels. He raises his arms.

ROMEO BEFORE THE CORPSE OF JULIET

FRIAR LAURENCE: Oh, perfect lovers!

CURTAIN

YOU DON'T HAVE TO COMPLICATE HAPPINESS

By Ramón Civedé

Adapted by MARCO DENEVI

MARCO DENEVI

CHARACTERS:

He
She

A park. Sitting on a stone bench under the trees, HE and SHE kiss.

HE: I love you.
SHE: I love you.
   They kiss again.
HE: I love you.
SHE: I love you.
   They kiss again.
HE: I love you.
SHE: I love you.
   HE stands up brusquely.
HE: That's enough! It's always the same thing! When I tell you I love you, why don't you say something different for a change, like… oh…, like you love somebody else?
SHE: Who?
HE: Nobody. You just say it so I'll be jealous. Jealousy is good for love. Being happy, the way we are, is too simple. We have to complicate it a little. Do you understand?
SHE: I didn't want to tell you because I didn't want you to be hurt. But now you've guessed it.
HE: What did I guess?
   SHE gets up and walks a few steps away.
SHE: That I love someone else.
   HE follows her.
HE: You're just saying that to please me. Because I asked you to.
SHE: No. I really do love somebody else.
HE: Who?
SHE: Someone.
   Silence.
HE: So, it's true then?
SHE: *(Sits down again. Sweetly.)* Yes, it's true.

YOU DON'T HAVE TO COMPLICATE HAPPINESS

HE paces back and forth. He pretends to be angry.

HE: I'm jealous. I'm not fooling. I'm jealous. I'm really jealous! I'd like to kill that guy.

SHE *(Sweetly):* He's over there.

HE: Where?

SHE: There, in the trees.

HE: I'm going to go look for him.

SHE: Be careful. He's got a gun.

HE: I'm not afraid.

HE goes off. Left alone, SHE laughs. A gunshot is heard. SHE stops laughing.

SHE: John.

Silence. SHE stands up.

SHE: John.

Silence. SHE runs toward the trees.

SHE: John.

Silence. SHE disappears into the trees.

SHE: John.

Silence. The stage is empty. Far away, her shattering scream is heard.

SHE: John!!

A few moments later, the curtain silently falls.

THE END

BLACK LIGHT

ÁLVARO MENÉN DESLEAL

ÁLVARO MENÉN DESLEAL

ALVARO MENÉN DESLEAL

El Salvador: 1932-2000

The author's real name was Alvaro Menéndez Leal. He used the pseudonym, Desleal (Disloyal), to indicate his dissent and opposition to much of what he observed and experienced. This trait showed up early in his life when, in 1952, he was expelled from school for writing and publishing a poem that authorities saw as "subversive." Continuing to write for publication, he was arrested the next year and accused of conspiring against the regime in power.

He spent some time as a boxer in Guatemala and Mexico, returning to El Salvador to continue his career as a writer. He also created two news programs for television. En 1961 he entered the University of El Salvador, while continuing to write prize-winning articles. The following year he was offered a lectureship at the university.

Menén Desleal was part of a writing group called "la generación comprometida" (the engaged [or committed] generation), influenced by the existentialist theories of Sartre. Well known as a dramatist, especially for his play *Luz negra (Black Light)*, he was also a poet and a writer of fantastic fiction.

His fortune fluctuated from government to government. He lived in exile for some time, and was also honored for his writings in his own country. While living abroad during El Salvador's civil war, he taught at universities in France, Germany and the United States.

His works have been translated into many languages (French, German, Portuguese, Danish, Romanian, Polish, and English). His best known work, *Luz negra*, written in 1964, has been performed in dozens of countries. The English translation of the *Black Light*, included in this anthology, was first published in *Drama and Theatre* in 1972.

BLACK LIGHT

All reason died at eleven o'clock last night.

H. Ibsen, *Peer Gynt,* Act IV, Scene XIII.

CHARACTERS:

Goter
Moter
A Blind Man
A Man, The Streetsweeper, A Little Girl.

Prologue

Darkness. Or a brightly lighted stage.
The Man enters. His head has been cut off, and his hands are tied behind his back. He delivers a monologue—which could just as well be coming from outer space— with a tone appropriate for someone telling a parable. He is suffering; but within that suffering we sense a joy—a joy which is not convincing. He moves with an easy, slow motion. Or he stands quite still. A moment of silence before he begins.

Once more—for the last time—the executioner sharpens the axe. I clench my fists from the cold and because, with his professional preoccupation with details, the executioner shows that he is guessing what I know as fact: that he is the man condemned to die. That I am the executioner.

Now, step by step, I climb the stairway to the scaffold. I do it slowly, deliberately, not simply because I have my hands tied behind my back, but also because with this slowness, this deliberateness, the executioner—my victim—suffers. When I reach the top, I pause and look around at the hungry, staring eyes of the crowd. I can see every expression in that sea of faces; but the executioner, in spite of the black mask that cries out his identity, can see only me.

And he is trembling. I know that he is trembling. He must hold the axe tightly in order to hide his shaking.

When I lean my chin against the clean wood surface, the executioner raises the blade and brings it down with great effort, without pause, without hesitation. My head rolls and my body falls limp; but his effort redeems me and enslaves my victim forever.

The executioner sees my blood and I fix my eyes on the sky.

Scene One

A gallows in the middle of the Square. Filth, blood and debris everywhere. It is just past noon, and the sun beats down on the setting. There are flies, flies everywhere. Goter lies on the platform, his head upright in one place, his body stretched out in another. He moves his eyes around in every direction possible. Down below on the pavement is Moter, in a similar position.

GOTER: Ha ha ha ha!
MOTER: *(Silence. He moves his eyes indifferently.)*
GOTER: Ha ha ha ha! They cut off your head!
MOTER: Idiot!
GOTER: Ha ha ha ha!
MOTER: I don't see why you should laugh. So they cut off my head... So what?
GOTER: Ha ha ha ha!
MOTER: Your head's cut off too!
GOTER: That's right... Ha ha ha! Mine's cut off too.
MOTER: So?
GOTER: I'm not laughing at me: I'm laughing at you. Ha ha ha ha! *(Little by little his laughter dies away. Silence.)*
MOTER: Sometimes, when I think that we could have...
GOTER: Shut up!
MOTER: Don't you feel well?
GOTER: What a question!... No, it isn't that I don't feel well, exactly... It's just that... with us here... like this...
MOTER: Come on! It's the best thing that could have happened to us... Swish! They cut off our heads, and when they did they cut off our problems too.
GOTER: That's right. So it's all over.
MOTER: Yes, it's all over. *(Silence).*

BLACK LIGHT

GOTER: Can you see your body?

MOTER: It's right in front of me.

GOTER: I can't see mine very well... I can just barely see my legs... It makes me a little sad to see those big shoes that won't carry me down the streets anymore... *(A change in mood.)* Ha ha ha ha!

MOTER: What are you laughing at now?

GOTER: Nothing, really. The bottom of one of my shoes has a hole in it. And it was that hole that made me fall... Just like the fable about the knight and the horseshoe.

MOTER: Are your legs the only part you can see?

GOTER: Yes, just my legs, almost up to the crotch... What about you? What can you see?

MOTER: Uh, I can see the whole thing!

GOTER: From your feet way up to your... neck?

MOTER: From my feet up to my neck.

GOTER: What does it look like?

MOTER: One of my arms is twisted under my body. I can't see the arm, but it hurts.

GOTER: Can I ask you something?

MOTER: Go ahead.

GOTER: ...Is your neck bleeding?

MOTER: Not anymore. I imagine most of the blood is up on the platform. How about you? Can you see any blood?

GOTER: Yes; quite a bit. It's all around me. But I don't know which is your blood and which is mine.

MOTER: Hmmm... I don't think that matters.

GOTER: But... the cut... Is it dry yet?

MOTER *(With repugnance)*: No; it isn't dry. A clear liquid is dripping out...

GOTER: That must be lymph.

MOTER: It must be what?

GOTER: Lymph.

MOTER: ...It's dripping slowly and steadily... The coagulated blood will stop it from flowing.

GOTER: What color is the blood that you see?

MOTER: It must be the same as it is up there. It's fairly black now.

GOTER: Does it stink?

MOTER: I don't know... I couldn't say. *(A pause.)* Are you looking at me?

GOTER: No. I'm not... Are you at me?
MOTER: No, I'm not either... That makes me feel lonely.
GOTER: Can you come up to the platform?
MOTER: Ha! Can you come down?
GOTER: No, I can't.
MOTER: Well, neither can I.
GOTER: The only thing I can move is my eyes.
MOTER *(Abruptly)*: Be quiet!
GOTER: What's the matter?
MOTER: I think someone's coming.
GOTER: Someone's coming here...?
MOTER: Yes; someone is coming here...
GOTER: Do you think they can hear us talking...?
MOTER: ...Them...?
GOTER: Yes, them... Do you suppose they can hear us?
MOTER: I imagine so.
GOTER *(Amused)*: Just think!
MOTER: Shhh!

They both wait expectantly. Footsteps are heard. They approach, stop, and then walk quickly away.

MOTER: They've gone away.
GOTER: Why?
MOTER: I don't suppose we're a very pretty sight.
GOTER: We frightened them.
MOTER: It's only natural. Dead people are frightening.
GOTER: Are we dead?
MOTER: Maybe... I don't know... Anyway, we're finished.
GOTER: Dead people don't talk.
MOTER: Do you really think we're talking?
GOTER: I hear you and you hear me!
MOTER: So, what does that mean?
GOTER: That's what talking is.
MOTER: Who knows?

A pause.

GOTER: There's one way to find out.
MOTER: What's that?
GOTER: It seems to me that if... when somebody comes along... No! Forget it!
MOTER: Come on! Tell me!

BLACK LIGHT

GOTER: It's too dangerous.

MOTER: They've already cut off our heads!

GOTER: If they find out we're talking, they could do something else to us.

MOTER: Nothing worse could happen to us now.

GOTER: They could burn us... Pour gasoline on us and set us on fire.

MOTER: It wouldn't change our situation.

GOTER: That's true. Nobody talks after it's all over.

MOTER: Tell me your plan.

GOTER: Okay... When somebody comes by, one of us should say something. If they hear us, then we're not dead.

MOTER (*Desperately*): And if they don't hear us?

GOTER: Well... then it's all over.

MOTER: That would mean...

GOTER: That would mean that we must be the way we are... Ha ha ha!

MOTER: Let's go ahead with the plan!

GOTER: All right. But remember, it's dangerous.

MOTER: What word shall we say?

GOTER: I don't know. Any one.

MOTER: Think of one. Just one.

GOTER: How about "love"?

MOTER: No. Not "love".

GOTER: "Water"... "bread"...

MOTER: Just one syllable would be good, a short word. It doesn't matter if it doesn't mean anything.

GOTER: "God"...

MOTER: An exclamation would be better.

GOTER: "Hey," "oh," "okay"...

MOTER: Some sound to fit the things around us.

GOTER: There's blood and filth all around us. Do you want the sound of blood?

MOTER: The "creaking" of the stairs up to the gallows...

GOTER: The "swish!" of the axe...

MOTER: Yes; the "swish!" of the axe...

GOTER: No; not that.

MOTER: Something! Think of something!

GOTER: "Love."

MOTER (*Annoyed*): All right; let's say "love." (*Silence.*) Oof! What a

picture! Two bloody heads saying "love"!
GOTER: What's wrong with that?
MOTER: It would be better to say "shit."
GOTER: It's not appropriate.
MOTER: Of course it's appropriate!
GOTER: It's not appropriate!
MOTER: Yes it is! We're surrounded by crap. Your head is in a pool of crap, and my neck is dripping crap!... That's why the flies are on us all the time! Flies don't go near altars, they hover around manure piles!
GOTER: All right. Don't get excited. We'll say "shit." (*A pause.*)
MOTER: ...I'm sorry... I got upset...
GOTER: Forget it.
MOTER: That was always my worst defect... The hole in your shoe made you fall... I had worse holes in my character. So forget what I said: we'll say "love."

Footsteps are heard.

GOTER: Someone's coming.
MOTER: Can you see them?
GOTER: No.
MOTER: Let's wait.

Silence. They are both listening.

MOTER *(Softly)*: He's taking a long time.
GOTER: *(Also softly.)* Quiet!

A pause. The Streetsweeper comes on stage, carrying a broom and a bucket of water. He walks slowly, tired, his head bowed, a half-smoked, unlit cigar hanging from his lips. He stops next to Moter's body, looks at it and gives it a little shove with his foot; then he goes over to the head. He puts the broom and bucket on the ground and painfully climbs up to the platform where he does the same thing that he did down below. He comes back down. He cleans the blood from his boots with the broom, and as he goes off, the broom in his hand, he takes the cigar out of his mouth and spits. A short pause.

MOTER: You idiot! You didn't say anything!
GOTER: I was waiting for *you*.
MOTER: That's what really makes me mad. We plan something, and then when the time comes to carry it out, we sit here like a couple of boobies.
GOTER: We didn't plan everything.
MOTER: Yes, we did.

GOTER: We didn't decide who would talk.

MOTER: What an excuse! Let's go over it again: if that human scum comes back...

GOTER: ...That scum who walks on his feet and has his head in place...

MOTER: Shut up! If he comes back, when he goes up to one of us, the other one will talk. Understand?

GOTER: No.

MOTER: If the man comes up to me, you'll talk; if he goes over to you, I'll talk. Got it?

GOTER: Got it.

MOTER: That way we'll confuse him. He'll think he's imagining things, and we'll find out if we can be heard.

GOTER: If he listens to us, we're alive.

MOTER: More or less.

GOTER: And if he doesn't?

MOTER: Idiot! He has to hear us!

GOTER: Why?

MOTER: Because he's alive, a human-being. He has ears, and we're talking.

GOTER: Maybe he won't be able to hear us... Maybe he's deaf or something.

MOTER: In that case, this farce will be over.

GOTER: And they'll bury us.

MOTER: That's what usually happens... And that scum, and the executioner, and all the rest of them will walk around in the sunlight—that sun we'll never see again.

GOTER: Do you regret it?

MOTER: ...No. I think the only objection I have is to the way they killed us.

GOTER: Wasn't the axe or the executioner to your satisfaction?

MOTER: Oh, I'm very happy with the service! The executioner knows his job, no doubt about it.

GOTER: Well, then?

MOTER: I mean that I was hoping death would meet me on another road...

GOTER: Ha ha ha! Pneumonia?

MOTER: It wouldn't have mattered; but I would have preferred to have been asleep. I think that's the best way... *(Thinking out loud.)* You're dreaming of something beautiful and, suddenly, a jab in your chest spins out the dream forever... In the morning, when they bring you your breakfast in bed, the maid, who has been walking on tip-toe so she won't disturb you, will come out of the bedroom screaming and knocking down furniture as she runs to call the lady of the house... "He croaked!" they'll both think, and you'll know that they both thought, "he croaked." Then your wife will come and cry over your body that's lying there, still warm, and she won't worry about staining her clothes or her hands the way she would if she came now.

GOTER: That's a dignified death.

MOTER: That's right. A decent death.

GOTER: Clean and decent. They even shave you, dress you up in your best suit and spray perfume on you. Really elegant.

MOTER: And then they have a family gathering. Friends come with flowers... And afterward they go along with you to the cemetery...

A pause.

GOTER: Why did it happen to you?

MOTER: Why did what happen to me?

GOTER: This... Your head...

MOTER: Oh, that!... Because I was stupid! It happens to us all because we're stupid!

GOTER: I suppose it was because of your political activities.

MOTER: I was never interested in politics. I was a crook.

GOTER: Did you kill anyone?

MOTER: No; I worked clean. In my business the main thing is to know that people would rather give up their life than their money; but they always hand over their money because they're vain.

GOTER: What about your conscience?

MOTER: Huh! A conscience is a sickness. I was always very healthy.

GOTER: That isn't true.

MOTER: A conscience depends on a man's stomach. *(A pause.)* I grew up very poor. My father was a laborer without any steady work: a stevedore, a janitor in a Danish slaughter-house... There were nine of us children, my mother was always sick and there wasn't enough money to pay the bills. My father brought scraps home from the meat market—guts, skin and blood—And that was our stew... It was then that I made up my mind never to go hungry again.

GOTER: You got rich.

BLACK LIGHT

MOTER: I didn't save a penny; but once in a while I had a fair amount of money. *(A change in mood.)* Ha ha ha! Once, on the Costa Brava, I fleeced the widow of a Yankee oilman!

GOTER: Didn't you ever care what the world thought?

MOTER: The world around us is a son of hunger... This filth and this blood are children of hunger too.

GOTER: But this isn't the only world...

MOTER: It's the only one we know.

GOTER: There's another one: a world of justice, a world of peace, a world of love...

MOTER: Oh, get off the love crap! If I'd had my choice, I wouldn't have taken a missionary for a traveling companion.

GOTER: I'm no missionary. I have plenty to complain about too.

MOTER: What, then?

GOTER: I never resigned myself to hope only in God. That's why I joined the Party.

MOTER: A party is a kind of god: it's all a bunch of promises for a later time.

GOTER: We didn't have many promises. It's just that I was tired of living in a muggy hole, of seeing my family starving to death, of seeing other people starving, and I decided to fight to make the world a better place.

MOTER: I'm sure you fought, but I don't think things have gotten any better.

GOTER: In a way... But let's not talk about that.

MOTER: Ha ha ha! Pardon me if I laugh: I'm beginning to like you. What's your name?

GOTER: Goter. What's yours?

MOTER: Moter.

GOTER: Moter? Our names sound alike.

MOTER: I have to tell you that this isn't my real name. I took the name of Moter because I thought it would make people trust me. "Nobody named Moter can be a bad man!" That's what those old ladies must have thought when they met me—those old ladies that I robbed blind later... Choosing a name is a thief's privilege—you know? Ha ha ha!

GOTER: And a revolutionary's: my name isn't really Goter either. Ha ha ha ha!

They both laugh happily.

ÁLVARO MENÉN DESLEAL

GOTER *(Serious)*: Moter!
MOTER *(Still laughing)*: What?
GOTER: One of my legs moved.
MOTER *(Serious)*: Are you sure?
GOTER: Uhhh… I don't know… Maybe I was wrong.
MOTER: Well, make sure.
GOTER *(Observing)*: No… I think I was wrong. *(A pause.)*
MOTER: What's the date today?
GOTER: I don't know. Do you have an appointment?
MOTER: I've always had one.
GOTER: And?
MOTER: And I met it. I went to it on the exact day and hour. But I still don't know the date today. I don't even know what year or what century this is.
GOTER: It's the year of Hitler. The Führer has taken over half the world.
MOTER: It's the year of the Losers. Christ has just lost Man.
GOTER: It's the year of Che Guevara.
MOTER: It's the year of Mao-Stalin.
GOTER: It's the year of… It is NOT the year of liberty.
MOTER: It is NOT the year of peace.
GOTER: It is NOT the year of democracy.
MOTER: It is NOT the year of the people.
GOTER: It is NOT the year of love.
MOTER: It is NOT your year or mine.
GOTER: …It is the year of death.
MOTER: It's the year of heads without men.
GOTER: It's the year of men without heads.
MOTER: *(A brief pause. A change of mood.)* Goter!
GOTER: What?
MOTER: My fingers moved.
GOTER: How?
MOTER: Like this… In jerks.
GOTER: Like they were trying to grab something?
MOTER: No; like they were trying to scare something away.
GOTER: Scare what away?
MOTER: Maybe flies. Yes; the fingers moved like they were trying to shake off flies.
GOTER: Then it's true—our bodies do move. *(A pause.)*

BLACK LIGHT

MOTER: Goter.

GOTER: What?

MOTER: ...What if our bodies, the same as our heads, weren't dead either.

GOTER: I don't believe it. The head is something special.

MOTER: Why is it something special?

GOTER: Well... Because of our brain. That's why.

MOTER: Because of our brain?

GOTER: Our heads carry *it* inside. They're like its carrying-case.

MOTER: Our bodies carry our heart.

GOTER: It's not the same thing.

MOTER: I know it's not the same, but it's important too.

GOTER: Yes, it is; but it isn't *as* important... it's just a simple muscle: it contracts... it expands... it contracts... it expands... until *pffft!* it bursts.

MOTER: It can't be that simple.

GOTER: If yours breaks down, they'll put another one in for you; but there's no one who can put in another brain.

MOTER: Whew! What pretty heads we have now. And independent too...

GOTER *(Abruptly)*: Shut up!

MOTER: Yes; they're really independent.

GOTER *(Softly and forcefully)*: Shut up!

MOTER: What is it?

GOTER: Listen.

They both listen.

MOTER: I don't hear anything.

GOTER: I thought I heard them laughing.

MOTER: At us?

GOTER: I don't know. They were laughing.

The laughter of a woman is heard. It is lusty, sensual laughter, and a man's laughter joins it. Then the woman's laughter continues alone.

MOTER: It's a young couple. Do you see them?

GOTER: No.

MOTER *(In an agonizing tone)*: What if it wasn't anyone?

GOTER: It's a man and a woman.

MOTER: What if it was God?

GOTER: Why God?

MOTER: I don't know... God laughing at us!

ÁLVARO MENÉN DESLEAL

The woman's laughter bursts out. It pervades everything, and the faces turn pale.
GOTER: They're coming!
The woman's laughter rings out over the stage itself, lustier than ever. Suddenly the laughter breaks off. Silence.
MOTER: Why did they stop?
GOTER: They saw us. They stopped cold when they saw us. *(Silence.)*
MOTER: They were laughing so happily.
GOTER: They were a couple of love-birds... Their laughter was sweet, so sweet! But they saw us and their happiness turned to horror.
MOTER: So, we cause horror then.
GOTER: Horror and disgust. That's what always happened to me: whenever I saw blood I felt like throwing up. What a strange liquid blood is! But now I'm satisfied: I don't have a stomach to worry about.
MOTER: What did she look like?
GOTER: Pretty. About twenty years old.
MOTER: Blonde?
GOTER: Brunette.
MOTER: What about him? What was he like?
GOTER: Strong: there was a woman at his side.
MOTER: Why were they laughing?
GOTER: They weren't laughing at us; they didn't even know we were here. When they saw us, a head here, a body over there, they stopped talking.
MOTER *(Abruptly)*: Shhh.
The man who was with the woman comes in. He looks at both of them; then he drapes a handkerchief over Moter's head, covering his face. He crosses himself, and goes out the same direction he came in.
GOTER: He's gone.
MOTER: Damn! He put a handkerchief on my head and it's covering up my eyes.
GOTER: A handkerchief?
MOTER: Yes, that idiot.
GOTER: Usually they cover bodies.
MOTER: I know; what a damned sweet thing to do!
GOTER: Does it make it hard to breathe?
MOTER: I'm not breathing. I can only make out a whitish glimmer of light.
GOTER: Don't be afraid; you should have faith.

BLACK LIGHT

MOTER: Have faith! Faith means to be afraid.

GOTER: At least the flies won't bother you now.

MOTER: I can feel them fluttering around on the handkerchief, and I hear the noise of their wings.

GOTER: You're better off than I am. They're on *my* nose; when they brush against my eyelids it's unbearable; I blink a lot to try to shoo them away; but they're intelligent, and they've already discovered what I am and all that I can do.

MOTER: Stick out your lower lip and blow on them.

GOTER *(Trying):* That's hard.

MOTER: It's not so hard. I've been doing it for a long time now; almost from the beginning.

GOTER: There was an audience then; the square was full of people and they would have noticed.

MOTER: When the people went away; when we were left alone.

GOTER: When the people went away the flies began to come, like limp crows.

MOTER: The people brought the flies.

GOTER: The flies came later.

MOTER: The people brought them. They always have flies around them.

GOTER: What a thought!

MOTER: It's disgusting… Thousands of eyes staring at me, and they would have liked to have burned me alive.

GOTER: They hated you.

MOTER: Maybe… When they brought you I had time to watch the mob's reactions better.

GOTER: What did you see?

MOTER: The same thing. When you came the eyes stared at you too…

GOTER: How did they look at me?

MOTER: Full of hate. They looked at you with hate. Every time the guards shoved you, the mob roared with approval. I've never seen people so happy!

GOTER: They weren't happy.

MOTER: They were! The people were glad to see you looking so pale and frightened, with your eyes bulging out. The ones nearest the gallows licked their lips with satisfaction when they saw you with your throat dry from fear.

GOTER: I wasn't afraid.

MOTER: It looked to me like you were afraid. But you ought to know. The people thought so too, and that's why they were so happy. People are sadistic.

GOTER: That's not true.

MOTER: They're not only sadistic; they're masochistic too. *(A brief pause.)* It's hard now to accept our own stupidity... Are you crying?

GOTER *(Trying to hide it):* No; I'm not crying.

MOTER: They executed us together because the people believe an idealist and a thief are the same thing, so they deserve the same punishment. If a guerrilla wins, he's a hero; if they capture him on a mountain he's an outlaw and they execute him.

GOTER: Don't go on.

MOTER: Maybe they're right. It's something more than using assumed names that puts a revolutionary and a common thief on equal footing. Thinking is an act of robbery... When they cut off heads, they're carrying out justice.

GOTER: This wasn't justice.

MOTER: It was their kind of justice anyway. That's what they call it: Justice with a capital "J". Did you read the circular that was being passed around the square during the executions?

GOTER: No.

MOTER: They said it there... Those bloody papers on the ground say it: it's justice that cut off our heads...

GOTER: Justice is blind.

MOTER: It isn't even one-eyed: it had pretty good aim when it swung the blade. And they killed us in the Square so that every eye would be a witness, so that they could make an example of us, to teach them that crime doesn't pay, that stealing is punished by death.

GOTER: I didn't steal.

MOTER: That thinking is punished by death.

GOTER: You're cruel.

MOTER: Our death was a spectacle. Or, even better, a lesson, a lesson for little children. That way the people learn that it's bad to steal, that it's bad to think. They're setting an example; but it's stupid to think about examples: I never thought about death when I was committing a crime. In fact, it was just the opposite. Whenever I swindled anyone I always felt a kind of fulfillment, a sort of sensual pleasure. Being a criminal, I know what I'm talking about: as a punishment, death is a myth, it's stupid. More than that, it's a glorification. The criminal reaches the peak of his career when he is condemned to die. It's then that his role as a villain becomes transformed into the role of a hero. Everyone talks about him; newsmen interview him, and children play at being the condemned man and the executioner; wooden axes cut off little heads... But if I, a criminal, feel a sensual pleasure when I commit a crime, the judge, the executioner and the spectators feel an even greater pleasure when the sentence is carried out, a sexual pleasure...

GOTER: *(Whistles a tune.)*
MOTER: Why are you whistling?
GOTER: So I won't hear you. I'm not bothering you, am I?
MOTER: It's not that you bother me; but it just isn't right.
GOTER: Come on; this business isn't so bad. (*Goter whistles and Moter blows on his handkerchief.*)
MOTER: See how afraid you are?
GOTER: What makes you think that?
MOTER: Because you're whistling. A man only whistles in two situations: when he's happy and when he's afraid. You're not happy.
GOTER: I could be.
MOTER: You aren't.
GOTER: It's no use pretending. No, I'm not happy. And I know you aren't either.
MOTER: I could be.
GOTER: You aren't.
MOTER: How do you know?
GOTER: Because you're talking. And words are what charlatans and prophets, believers and swindlers use...
MOTER: I'm a swindler.
GOTER: You're a dead man. *(A pause.)*
MOTER: Where did you die, Goter?
GOTER: I don't know; what about you?
MOTER: I don't know either.
GOTER: So: we died in the same place. *(A pause.)*
MOTER: It's terrible. No one's coming.
GOTER: What do you want people for?
MOTER: Christ! You know: the plan...
GOTER: That's right: the plan. I forgot. *(A brief pause.)*
MOTER: Are you forgetful?
GOTER: No. I always had an excellent memory. In school I learned

pages and pages of poetry by heart. I can still recite it.
(He recites):
"I know that I am deathless,
I know this orbit of mine cannot be swept by a carpenter's compass,
I know I shall not pass like a child's carlacue cut with a burnt stick at night.
I know I am august,
I do not trouble my spirit to vindicate itself or be understood.
I see that the elementary laws...
(He hesitates.) The elementary laws...
I see that the elementary laws..." Bah!

MOTER: That's a sign.

GOTER: Learning poetry?

MOTER: No; forgetting.

GOTER: A sign of what?

MOTER: A sign of... *(He breaks off the sentence; a change in mood.)* You begin by forgetting; for a little while, that's all... Then comes a strange, vivid, fleeting review of your entire life... Then, nothingness.

GOTER: Do you believe that?

MOTER: That's what they always told me... The most childish and far away details of our lives come into our mind: the apple we stole from a neighbor; the day we ran off from school; the lie we told our girlfriend that afternoon when... Everything, like in a motion picture, with its smallest details, with its most intimate shimmers and shadows...

GOTER: Have you started to forget?

MOTER (Smiling): I remember one time in Central America when I was a great coffee dealer. I took a strange name that sounded Hindu... *(Almost gleeful.)* I put an announcement in the newspapers saying that the purpose of my trip was to make big business deals. I showed letters, bank accounts, credentials, everything; but the way I convinced them I was rich, more than anything else, was with the receptions I held in the Balmoral Hotel. As if they'd never been swindled before! I gave parties for the coffee growers, for the cotton brokers, the bankers, the government ministers... Business deals were made by the light of champagne. I bought six million dollars worth of coffee, I signed I.O.U.'s, and I asked them to send that aromatic fruit of their labors to an English port, in my name...

BLACK LIGHT

In England I sold the coffee at a tremendous loss: I gave it away for less than two million dollars. Then I disappeared... Ha ha ha ha!

GOTER: Weren't you ever caught?

MOTER: No. The other four million was used to make me invisible... It was the best job I ever pulled, ha ha ha! A bank was on the verge of going broke!

GOTER: Yes, that was quite a job, all right.

MOTER: They're still looking for me. *(A pause.)*

GOTER: Moter.

MOTER: What?

GOTER: You changed the subject.

MOTER: What were we talking about?

GOTER: The plan.

MOTER: That's right. The plan. *(Silence.)*

GOTER: It's terrible.

MOTER: Terrible.

GOTER: No one's coming.

MOTER: That man will come back now.

GOTER: Or somebody who's curious.

MOTER: But it's getting late.

GOTER: It will be night soon; but still, there's always the hope of a straggling drunk.

MOTER: It's strange that no one's coming by. The Square is usually the most crowded place in the city.

GOTER: I took part in demonstrations in this Square. When "this" happened to us today, it made me feel like I was at a demonstration.

MOTER: Did you used to speak in public?

GOTER: Sometimes. Later on, when the situation became critical, no speeches were needed.

MOTER: And then?

GOTER: It was time to act.

MOTER: What did you people do?

GOTER: Everything: we had underground newspapers printed up on a mimeograph machine; bombs, Molotov cocktails...

MOTER: What were you trying to do with them?

GOTER: Take control.

MOTER: I didn't think you were ambitious.

GOTER: It wasn't for me: it was for the people, for the Party.

MOTER: Oh!

GOTER: And why not? A Party that doesn't try to take over is a charity, a group of Boy Scouts, a club for useless old men… It's whatever you like, except a Party.
MOTER: And were you successful?
GOTER: No. If we'd been successful, I wouldn't be here.
MOTER: You'd be safe.
GOTER: I'd be in control, which is another kind of danger. There would be other men here.
MOTER: Your enemies.
GOTER: The enemies of the people.
MOTER: Those people who were so glad to see you die.
GOTER: They weren't glad… Tomorrow you'll see how those people go to the cemetery of their heroes.
MOTER: Bull! People go to cemeteries to bury the dead, and to make love… The place I think the people will go is to the Square, where someday they'll put up a statue to you: a beautiful, upright head…
GOTER: I think you're going too far.
MOTER: …Sorry. I didn't mean to offend you.

Silence. Moter blows on his handkerchief

GOTER: How do you feel?
MOTER. I don't know… I'm losing strength little by little.
GOTER: Are you going to faint?
MOTER: No. But when I blow on the handkerchief, it's like I don't have enough strength to make it move as much as before.
GOTER: Your windpipe must have gotten plugged up with coagulated blood.
MOTER: Maybe… But… what if we're dying?
GOTER: We were always dying.
MOTER: I mean right now. What if our souls are really leaving our bodies…?
GOTER: Then, it will all be over.
MOTER: We have to shout.
GOTER: What for?
MOTER: So they'll hear us.
GOTER: No one will hear us.
MOTER: Somebody has to hear us! They have to!
GOTER: It's useless.
MOTER: No; let's practice the word.
GOTER: Shit?

MOTER: Love… Are you ready?
GOTER: Ready.
MOTER: As loud as we can. Maybe they'll hear us…
GOTER: Maybe…
MOTER: I'll count to three.
GOTER: All right.
MOTER: One… two…
GOTER: Wait a minute.
MOTER: What's wrong?
GOTER: Nothing; but let's not shout at the same time.
MOTER: Why not?
GOTER: So we can listen to each other. So that we can correct each other.
MOTER Okay. Ready?
GOTER: Ready.
MOTER: You shout first.
GOTER: All right.
MOTER: One… two… three!
GOTER *(Not very loudly)*: Love.
MOTER: Love.
GOTER: Love.
MOTER *(Louder)*: Love!
GOTER *(Just as loud)*: Love!
MOTER *(Very loud)*: Love!
GOTER *(At the top of his lungs)*: Love!
MOTER *(The same way)*: Love!

They keep shouting, miserably, hopefully. A cold wind blows, stirring up the filth and bloody circulars. A long, heavy silence while Goter looks down and Moter does not blow on his handkerchief

MOTER: Nobody?
GOTER: Nobody.
MOTER: It's terrible.
GOTER: Terrible.

Scene Two

ÁLVARO MENÉN DESLEAL

It has grown dark. There is no longer a wind. Moter blows stubbornly on his handkerchief.

GOTER: Ha ha ha ha!
MOTER: *(Blowing on the handkerchief)*
GOTER: Ha ha ha ha!
MOTER: What are you laughing at?
GOTER: At the way you're blowing. Did the handkerchief fall off?
MOTER: No; it's still on my—head… Still on me.
GOTER: It's getting cool.
MOTER: Has it gotten dark?
GOTER: Yes; it's almost nighttime.
MOTER: So much the better. The sun burned the skin on my face. It hurts.
GOTER *(Amused):* It really roasted mine; you have a parasol! Ha ha ha ha!
MOTER: You irk me more than the handkerchief does.
GOTER: How are your flies doing?
MOTER: They're not flitting around anymore. Some of them have stayed behind to sleep on my head.
GOTER: You're nothing but a head.
MOTER: There's one consolation…
GOTER: What?
MOTER: My corns won't hurt me anymore.
GOTER: Anyway, your handkerchief is a shield. The flies don't bother you the way they do me.
MOTER: I'll trade you my handkerchief for your flies.
GOTER: A while ago a couple of flies had intercourse on my nose.
MOTER: Ha! What an uncomfortable wedding bed!
GOTER: Still, when they were going through the sexual act, I noticed their satisfaction, the lecherous shine in their myriads of eyes, the orgasm in the vibration of their wings…
MOTER: You should have called them names.
GOTER: No. They were seminating flies like they were at the gates of a temple. They wanted my blessing.
MOTER: Do they have it?
GOTER: They have it. I hope with all my heart that their coitus will lead to the birth of infinite generations of virile males and prolific females… A small breath of my spirit will live on in them. Though

I die, my spirit will live on!

MOTER: Oh Great Father and Grandfather of Flies, tell me: Can you see the sky?

GOTER: Yes, I can. It's clear. Clear and black.

MOTER: Then you must be able to see the Southern Cross; it's my favorite constellation...

GOTER: No, I don't see it... *(A pause; softly.)* I think someone's coming.

MOTER: The man?

GOTER: I don't know. He has a light in his hands. Lanterns.

MOTER: It must be an angel.

GOTER: Ssshhhh!

MOTER *(Softly)*: The plan!

GOTER: Ssshhhh!

The Little Girl comes in, she is carrying lighted candles. She places some of them on the ground around Moter's body, and then she places others around Goter's body. She crosses herself and as she removes the handkerchief from Moter she runs off, terrified. A pause.

MOTER: The plan, the plan!

GOTER: It was a little girl.

MOTER: I know; she took the handkerchief off me. But I don't care if she was a little girl; we should have said something to her.

GOTER: I'm sorry. I couldn't do it.

MOTER: Neither could I.

GOTER: It's strange.

MOTER: I told you it was an angel.

GOTER: It wasn't an angel.

MOTER: You can't be sure.

GOTER: They say that angels are made of light and fire. It was just a little girl carrying candles in her hands.

MOTER: It was an angel who took the form of a little girl.

GOTER: Why of a little girl? It could have been of a little boy.

MOTER: Angels are hermaphrodites.

GOTER: Angel or girl, we should have said something to her. I think we were stupid again.

MOTER: Forget it; fate decides better than we do. The man will come now.

GOTER: I don't think he'll come.

MOTER: He'll come; it's his job. He brought a broom like Saint Martin of Porres, and he left his bucket at the foot of the gallows. That

means he'll come back to wash up the blood.
GOTER: They should have cleaned up a long time ago. They've abandoned us. They've left the city!
MOTER: Someone has to come. Men bury their corpses.
GOTER: So, the gravediggers will come. By that time it will be too late.
MOTER: It won't be too late.
GOTER: Yes, it will. We'll be dead. The gravediggers will come, and by then we won't be able to talk to them.
MOTER: Do you feel sick?
GOTER: I've gotten a little weaker. My ears are ringing.
MOTER: Mine too.
GOTER: You said the little girl took the handkerchief off you.
MOTER: Yes; and I'm grateful. Now I can see the candles around my body. Thank you, little girl or angel, for giving me this funereal spectacle!
GOTER: It was an act of piety.
MOTER: I can see the candles that she put around you too. The picture you offer isn't a very cheery one either; but it makes me feel better anyway; I can see part of you now. Before I couldn't see anything but the empty Square, and your voice that kept coming to me from off in the distance, out of the wind, out of the sky. That made me afraid. Now I feel as though you are those little flames, those tiny wicks, subject to the whim of a breath of air.
GOTER: Maybe that's what I am. Those flames are the only thing left of us: so weak and defenseless, as defenseless and weak as we always were. A little puff of wind and it's all over.
MOTER: God is unmerciful.
GOTER: Stop thinking. Don't think.
MOTER: My self goes away, and I don't know where. God is not the God of the dead, but of the living. Well, anyway I have a pigsty reserved for me in hell.
GOTER: You've got to have faith.
MOTER: I don't want to see God. The Bible says that whoever sees God will die. My only desire is to go on living this life that's slipping away from me.
GOTER: God is just, and we are his children.
MOTER: That's going too far. We are mere dreams in his nightmare, and now God is waking up.
GOTER: It doesn't matter. In us there breathes the spirit of future

generations.

MOTER: Even if they're flies. Ha! You said it: we're food for worms…

GOTER: *(Whistles a tune.)*

MOTER: You're whistling again.

GOTER: Yes; so I won't hear you. And so I won't hear myself either.

A pause. Goter whistles. We hear the tapping of a cane on the ground. Goter stops whistling. Silence.

GOTER: Did you hear that?

MOTER: Yes.

GOTER: They're hitting something.

A pause. They listen.

MOTER: It's… like they're hammering.

GOTER: They must be making our coffins.

MOTER: They're dragging something along the Square.

GOTER: Let's wait.

A pause. The noise of the cane comes nearer.

MOTER *(Softly)*: It's a blind man. Let's say the word to him.

GOTER *(Softly)*: It won't work.

MOTER: Why not?

GOTER: Blind men and dogs can hear the voices of the dead.

The Blindman comes onstage with a mongrel dog.

MOTER: That's stupid. Let's talk to him. If we don't, he'll bump into my head. *(To the Blindman.)* Oh, Sir!

The Blindman stops to listen.

GOTER: Good evening, Mr. Blindman.

BLINDMAN *(As if to himself)*: There are two people here. Two men.

GOTER: You're right. There are two of us.

MOTER: We don't know if we're people or not.

GOTER: We don't know if we're men.

BLINDMAN: Two people. Two men. I am the blindman.

GOTER: We see that. What's your name?

BLINDMAN: Blindman.

GOTER: I asked you your name.

BLINDMAN: Blindman, that's all. When you lose the light, you lose the name; when the name is lost, the man is lost.

MOTER: You have a beautiful dog.

BLINDMAN: Nothing is beautiful. Nothing exists.

MOTER: I can see his bearing and his coat.

ÁLVARO MENÉN DESLEAL

BLINDMAN: I wouldn't care if he were scabby. He's my friend, that's all.

MOTER: I'd say he's an Afghan. They're good runners.

GOTER: I'd say he's the Dog Howling at the Moon by Juan Miró. There's a ladder, a ladder that reaches the sky; the master is up above, high up... If someone tries to climb the ladder, the dog barks and the master stops them from going up.

BLINDMAN: I would prefer him to be the dog of Spinoza: mute, like the dogs the Spanish conquerors found in America. That kind of dog lets you go up the ladder, or, at least try to.

MOTER: He looks like an Afghan to me. I've seen them run on hundreds of dog-racing tracks.

BLINDMAN: Whatever he is, we're friends, partners; we've established a symbiosis. He lends his eyes to see; I lend my empty sockets to move people to charity. We split the profits. *(He makes a motion as if to sit down.)*

MOTER: Wait! Don't sit there... It's dirty.

BLINDMAN: What's there?

MOTER: Mud and debris... If you want to sit down, I'll help you.

BLINDMAN: Give me your hand.

MOTER: N-no... I can't. My hands are full; but follow my instructions, and I'll guide you to a seat.

BLINDMAN: All right.

MOTER *(Giving instructions to the Blindman)*: Turn a little to your left... There!... Now take four steps forward... One more step. That's it. You can touch the stairs of a platform with your cane. Sit down there.

BLINDMAN: Thank you. *(He sits down. Silence.)*

GOTER: Where did you come from?

BLINDMAN: Far away.

GOTER: Where?

BLINDMAN: Far away. I never know where I am, what town I'm passing through or where I'm going.

GOTER: Were you born blind?

BLINDMAN: No. I remember blue and red very well... women's faces, the leaves on the trees in autumn... Twilight, the stars...

GOTER: Was it in an accident?

BLINDMAN: What?

GOTER: The way you lost your sight.

BLACK LIGHT

MOTER: Maybe it was because of an illness. In the southwest of Mexico I saw whole families of blind people. Onchocerciasis had made their eyes burst.

BLINDMAN: It wasn't an accident or illness. My sight... they stole it from me.

GOTER: They stole it from you?

MOTER: Huh? Can you tell us what you mean?

BLINDMAN: I always do. It's my revenge. Whenever I tell this story, I imagine that I'm a living manifesto, a declaration that discloses its truths. *(He takes out a pack of cigarettes and offers it.)* Cigarette?

GOTER: Uhh... I don't smoke.

MOTER: I'd like to, but they don't agree with me. You know: the nicotine, lung cancer...

GOTER: Thanks anyway. Tell us your story.

BLINDMAN *(In a strange tone, caught up)*: It happened in Africa. In Algiers... I was fighting for the liberation... For several months we made some good strikes; I blew up two electric plants myself... One day, while we were planning the destruction of a radio station in Hassi-Messaoud, the French fell on us... They took me and my wife to a prison in the desert... They tried to make us talk, they even tortured us... My wife—oh, God, I'll never forget it!—they stuck a bottle into her organ to make her talk. She bled a lot. Blood didn't bother them. One day they took her somewhere else, I don't know where, and I never saw her again... One afternoon, twenty days after I'd been captured, a sergeant—a paratrooper—came to my cell. "The captain wants to see you," he said to me. "All right," I answered... We went to his office. The captain offered me a cigarette... He tried to make me talk by being kind, by flattering me, by offering me bribes... That only made me laugh... The captain became furious... I kept laughing... He threatened to gouge out my eyes. I knew he was capable of it, but I kept laughing... Then while the sergeant twisted my arm behind my back, he shoved me around and made me look at the walls of his office. "I'm going to give your eyes their last little bit of amusement," he said, almost as though he were playing, while he forced me to look at the pictures hanging on the walls... There was a calendar with a picture of Brigitte Bardot on it. "Masturbate in your mind," he told me; "it's the last time you'll ever see her." I looked away. I did like to look at her, it's true, and I went to the theater to see her movies whenever I could; but this time it was completely different... *(He stands up.)* It seemed to me then that that picture was the very image of France, and I thought that in the captain's mind that girl's legs were more important than Marseilles, than France itself... "Look at the Arch of Triumph," he said to me; "and the Eiffel Tower." I kept looking away. "Look at the Moulin Rouge," he shouted, shoving the picture in my face; "you won't even remember the windmill there anymore." I didn't say a word. "You people are swine," he roared while he was pushing me over to his chair; "I'm going to gouge your eyes out..." The sergeant tied me up and stood at one side, seeing and trying not to see. "I'll leave you the pits!" And, seething, he said to me: "Swine. That's what you are... You'll never bring the glory of France to an end..." He threw himself at me... For a split second I thought about the nude on the calendar... I couldn't move... His thumbs disgorged my eyes... Blood running down my face, my sockets are left empty, the light explodes, there is no light...! *(A pause.)* Then I laughed for the last time. *(He sits down.)*

GOTER: That's a terrible story.
MOTER: Yes; it's horrible.
BLINDMAN: Sometimes I think of committing suicide.
GOTER: That's not a very desirable solution.
MOTER: A man has to live. To live!
GOTER: We all think about suicide some time. When that happens we become adults.
BLINDMAN: I would prefer death. I can only wait.
GOTER: I was saved from suicide because of political curiosity.
MOTER: I was saved because I was afraid I might hurt myself.

A pause.

BLINDMAN: It's getting cool; is it going to rain?
GOTER: I don't think so. The sky is clear.
BLINDMAN: You mentioned a platform. What kind of platform is it?
MOTER: Oh, a platform for public events.
BLINDMAN: So we're in a Square.
MOTER: Yes; it's a Public Square. It's empty today.
BLINDMAN: The platform must be used for speeches.
MOTER: Not exactly.
BLINDMAN: What did they build this one for?
MOTER: Well... for a certain very—important—public event.
BLINDMAN: A lot of well dressed people must have come, public

officials, military bands.

MOTER: The most important public officials were a judge and an executioner. And as for the people, they stank.

BLINDMAN: Hmmm… What kind of public event?

MOTER: You tell him, Goter.

GOTER: Well… two executions.

BLINDMAN: Did they shoot two criminals?

MOTER: They didn't shoot them; they cut off their heads.

GOTER: With an axe. The executioner came, and he cut off the two heads with a sharp axe.

BLINDMAN: Criminals and generals die with their boots on.

MOTER: One of them was an idealist. He thought a lot.

BLINDMAN: So they killed him?

MOTER: Yes. They would have liked to have killed him a hundred times.

BLINDMAN: And the other one?

MOTER: He was…

GOTER *(Interrupting him):* He was a citizen.

BLINDMAN: Did he think too?

GOTER: Yes; he thought too. He found it out too late, but he thought too.

BLINDMAN: This is a strange place; what do they call it?

MOTER: It would be better if you didn't have it in your mind to remember.

BLINDMAN: But do they give the death penalty here to people who think?

MOTER: Why not? It's a crime like any other one.

GOTER: It's common in many parts of the world. The same thing happened to you. But in this case it wasn't simply that they thought. To be honest, they were swindlers too.

MOTER: Actually, only one of them was a swindler.

GOTER: I think they both were.

BLINDMAN: I can understand your uncertainty. There is no absolutely sure way to distinguish a saint from a hoodlum. Were they friends?

MOTER: Only at the last minute.

BLINDMAN: When they were captured.

MOTER: No; later. They got to know each other at the moment of death.

ÁLVARO MENÉN DESLEAL

BLINDMAN: If they had known each other before, they would still be alive.
GOTER: That wasn't their destiny.
MOTER: Their destiny was carried out. We were meant to meet each other, and we met; no later, no earlier, but at the exact place and time.
BLINDMAN *(Standing up)*: But you're talking about yourselves!
GOTER: Don't get excited. We're talking about the men who were executed.
BLINDMAN: Why did they kill them in the Square?
MOTER: So that they would be an example. If you'd like, I'll read the handout they were circulating today; it tells about their crimes.
BLINDMAN: Read it.
MOTER: You'll have to get it for me; there are a lot of them on the ground.
BLINDMAN: Can't you get it?
MOTER: No; but I'll tell you where it is.
BLINDMAN: *(Follows Moter's instructions until he picks up a bloody paper.)*
BLINDMAN: This paper feels strange.
MOTER: It's dirty; it has mud on it. *(He gives him directions for putting the paper on the ground, next to his eyes.)* Walk a little to the left... That's it. Now, three steps forward... Okay. Put the paper on the ground.
BLINDMAN: On the ground?
MOTER: On the ground.
BLINDMAN: Are you crippled?
MOTER: In a way; part of my body is missing.
BLINDMAN: A war casualty.
MOTER *(Laughing)*: A peace casualty. *(The Blindman puts the paper in front of Moter's face.)* You have it upside down; turn it over.
BLINDMAN *(Turning the paper over)*: Sorry. *(He sits down again.)*
MOTER: All right.
GOTER: I haven't seen what you're going to read either. Is it the circular you told me about?
MOTER: That's the one.
GOTER: I'm curious to know how they justified the executions.
MOTER: You'll find out now. Listen. *(He reads the paper. While he is reading the Blindman becomes agitated, filled with anguish.)*
Here, or anywhere, anyplace at all,
the Time doesn't matter, if it is today or if it was yesterday,

nor do the means or the methods;
if the race is white or black,
if the men are Bantu or British,
because they don't matter either.
I say that it is only important for birds to fly,
I say it is important for children to keep their open happiness,
I say that it is important for little girls to play ring around the rosy,
I say it is important for there to be many dolls,
and that little lead soldiers are more important than real soldiers,
and more important than bells on churches and on schools.
I say that the sheet of cheap paper on which the boy writes his simple words of love
to the country girl, is more important than manifestos and political declarations
That the yellowed photograph on which the mother keeps the image of her son who did not come back from the war
is more important than the photograph of the public official,
than the photograph of the official's wife,
than the photograph of the official's dog and his house full of servants...

BLINDMAN *(Gets to his feet violently, strikes his cane on the ground and shouts):* That's enough!

MOTER: Why? Aren't you convinced?

BLINDMAN: You tricked me. You read a city ordinance declaring that the dogs that accompany blind men must be killed!

MOTER: You're crazy! I read the accusations against the men who were executed. My friend heard them.

GOTER: I heard something else.

MOTER: You're both in this against me. I read an insulting manifesto.

GOTER: I heard a song of liberty and peace.

BLINDMAN: What a strange town. They kill dogs and thinkers. I'm leaving. *(He takes a few steps.)*

GOTER: Goodbye.

BLINDMAN *(Stops):* Excuse me... Don't get angry... I take it that one of you can't walk. It seems to me that we could join forces.

MOTER: Do you want us to set up a bank? An airline?

GOTER: Cut it out, Moter; let him finish.

BLINDMAN: Uhh... I'm strong; I could carry the crippled one on my shoulders. I'll use my feet, he'll use his eyes.

ÁLVARO MENÉN DESLEAL

MOTER: We can't. We have to stay here.

GOTER: Very nice of you; but we have to leave soon on a far away mission.

BLINDMAN: Well then, goodbye. *(He takes a step, and then stops.)* Uhh... Excuse me again. My question may sound impertinent to you; but people don't talk to me very often...

GOTER: Don't worry; ask anything you like.

MOTER *(In an even tone, without any stresses):* Winter is especially raw today... Winter is especially raw today... A blanket of snow covers all of Europe... It has snowed in places where it never snowed before... In the South, far to the South, in the Canary Islands... Paris, 20 degrees; London, 15 degrees; Brussels, 10 degrees; Copenhagen, 12 degrees; Geneva, 5 degrees; Moscow, 8 degrees below zero... Winter is especially raw today...especially raw... raw...

BLINDMAN: What are you saying?

MOTER: Me? Nothing; I haven't said a word. I'm waiting for your question.

BLINDMAN: Uhh... I'd like to know the name of this Square. My curiosity probably seems strange to you; but, in a way, I'm a collector.

MOTER: What do you collect? Stamps?

BLINDMAN: I collect names of Squares. The heart of a city is in them. I know the names of many of the Squares in the big cities. I'm an expert in that sort of thing. I... I could even guess the name of this Square.

GOTER: Tell us what you think it's called.

BLINDMAN: Every city has a Square with this name. Although it's true that some Squares aren't necessarily the heart of a city. It's generally thought that they are its lungs; but they could be its liver, its stomach, its ass. The leaders of a town don't call it a liver, a stomach or an ass: they call it a heart. That's why they always have a Square with this name.

MOTER: Heart Square?

BLINDMAN: No; Liberty Square. This Square is called Liberty Square.

GOTER: You're wrong.

BLINDMAN: Then, what is its name?

GOTER: Liberty Square.

BLINDMAN: Liberty Square. I never would have thought it. It should be called Liberty Square.

BLACK LIGHT

GOTER: Still, it's called Liberty Square.
MOTER: Liberty? I thought its name was Liberty Square.
GOTER: No; it's Liberty Square, which is still ironic. That's why, when the Party comes to power, they'll change its name.
BLINDMAN: What will they call it?
GOTER: Liberty Square.
BLINDMAN: I think that's a better name for it. Goodbye. *(He goes off.)*
MOTER: Goodbye.
GOTER: Goodbye.
A pause so the Blindman can leave.
MOTER *(Exhilarated):* He heard us!
GOTER: I told you, it won't work with him.
MOTER: It has to work!
GOTER: I already told you. *(A pause.)*
MOTER: So then, we played the part of ghosts.
GOTER: More or less.
MOTER: We should be careful. It's not good to play ghosts.
GOTER: That's true. Cabalists say that by playing ghosts we could turn into ghosts.
MOTER: What shall we do now?
GOTER: Wait. It will only work with the man.
MOTER: It's no use.
GOTER: You'll see: it will work.
MOTER: The man is deaf. He won't hear our word.
GOTER: Let's wait.
Silence.
MOTER: It's awful.
GOTER: Yes; it's awful.
MOTER: Nobody's coming.
GOTER: They're all at home.
MOTER: They got there, sated with emotions, they watched television a while, and then they went to bed on top of their wives.
GOTER: The man will come to clean up the blood.
MOTER: The gravediggers will come to take us away. *(A pause.)* And if you were given another chance… *(A pause. Goter is silent.)*… Would you do the same things? *(Goter doesn't answer.)* Goter! *(Loudly, in desperation.)* Goter!
GOTER: What?
MOTER: I asked you a question.

GOTER: Uh, sorry; I didn't hear you. I think my mind is starting to go. What did you ask me?
MOTER: I asked you if you would do the same things if you were given another chance.
GOTER: I don't know. I really don't know now. What about you?
MOTER: Well… I don't know either. Everything is becoming less clear to me. *(A short pause.)* I really did have some good times. *(He smiles.)* I was in the war in Africa too.
GOTER: A rebel?
MOTER: No; on the side of the French… I joined the Legion. When I had leave I would walk along the elegant streets and stop to look at ladies' underthings in the shops and stores… What tiny, delicate little things!... Then I'd go off to the whorehouses.
GOTER: You said you never killed anyone.
MOTER: Maybe because I didn't have time for it; one day I ran off with a black dancer, and I never went back to the war.

A pause.

GOTER: Who gouged the blindman's eyes out?
MOTER: The Yankees. He said it happened in Vietnam.
GOTER: No; he said it was in Algiers.
MOTER: In Vietnam.
GOTER: In Algiers.
MOTER: I'm positive. He said it very clearly: it was in Algiers.
GOTER: In Vietnam.
MOTER: In Algiers.
GOTER: In Cuba! It was in Cuba!
MOTER: Cuba doesn't have anything to do with it. It was in the Six Days War.
GOTER: In the Dominican Republic. The Yankees always do it.
MOTER: You're stupid. The Arabs gouged out his eyes when they invaded Israel.
GOTER: That never happened. The Jews gouged out his eyes; that's what he said.
MOTER: It was in Biafra.
GOTER: Not Biafra; Bolivia. It was the Bolivian army. The blindman's name is Debray.
MOTER: He said his name was Dutschke. He lost his sight when a bullet wounded him in the head in Berlin.
GOTER: It was Cohn Bendit. De Gaulle ordered him to be blinded

with acid in the May Revolution.

MOTER: He didn't tell us his name. He said he had been in Prague, and that his name was simply Blindman.

GOTER: It was in China.

MOTER: The Green Berets did it. In Guatemala Brazil Panama Spain –Greece Portugal.

GOTER: Whatever you say; but it was on Earth.

MOTER: Don't be so sure.

GOTER: What blind man are you talking about?

MOTER: I'm not talking about any blind man. I'm talking about a calendar with a nude picture of Brigitte Bardot.

A pause.

GOTER: Do you feel something strange?

MOTER: I don't get you.

GOTER: I asked if you felt something strange; something… I don't know.

MOTER: No. Why do you ask?

GOTER: Well… I feel something strange.

MOTER: Are you in pain?

GOTER: No; I don't hurt. I just feel strange, as though I were less tangible.

MOTER: So, everything's about to come to an end; and yet, I should feel the symptoms before you do.

GOTER: Why?

MOTER: Because it happened to me first. You stayed behind, intact, on the platform longer.

GOTER: That's right. I was last.

MOTER: You lived longer.

GOTER: I suffered longer.

MOTER: That's why I should feel the symptoms before you.

GOTER: I don't know. When the axe blade cut through the bones in your neck, it sounded like a dry branch on a tree. When your head rolled I thought the world was rolling. I suffered for you and for me. They killed me twice!

A pause.

MOTER: What if we tried to put our heads back on…?

GOTER: How?

MOTER: Move them over to the bodies; put them on the shoulders.

GOTER: We can't.

ÁLVARO MENÉN DESLEAL

MOTER: Someone could! The blindman could!
GOTER: It wouldn't do any good. Our bodies won't move anymore.
MOTER: So, you've lost all hope.
GOTER: Yes, I have. And I'm resigned.
MOTER: And what about the plan?
GOTER: It's no use; they won't hear us.
MOTER: We have to shout! We have to!
GOTER: You do it if you want. I just want to rest.
MOTER: Both of us! We both have to say something!
GOTER: I can't. I feel weak.
MOTER: Try! Do it for me, your friend!
GOTER *(Mollified):* Do you hear music?
MOTER: Music?
GOTER: Far away... Pleasant...
MOTER: What kind of music?
GOTER: Verdi's *Requiem.* Listen.

Silence.

MOTER: I don't hear anything.
GOTER: Very far away... very far... One day I heard it in Antigua, Guatemala; it was in a church demolished by earthquakes, but magnificent in its ruins. Orchestras from all the Central American countries had come, and there was a chorus of five hundred voices... Yes, five hundred voices, and some magnificent soloists...! In back of us, facing the orchestra, far off, as though from heaven, the Trumpets of the Last Judgment... Very far away! Very far! *(Silence. Goter gives a terrible shout.)* Spirit of God!
MOTER: Goter, Goter!

Silence.

GOTER *(Shouting with all his might):* Spirit of God!
MOTER: Goter, Goter! Dear Goter!
GOTER: Don't get excited; I was listening to the Requiem.
MOTER: You scared me... I can't imagine myself alone here... The idea that you may die terrifies me.
GOTER: We'll both die.
MOTER: No, Goter; you shouldn't die. Let me die! *(Silence.)* Whistle, Goter! Whistle the tune! I want to hear you!
GOTER: *(Smiles, and whistles a while.)*
MOTER: Goter.
GOTER: Yes; I heard it.

BLACK LIGHT

Footsteps are heard.

MOTER: The man, it's the man! We're saved, Goter! God didn't forget us!

GOTER: The word!

MOTER: Love, Goter; love!

Verdi's Requiem begins to play softly. The Streetsweeper enters, and sweeps up the loose paper and debris.

MOTER *(Softly):* Now, Goter; now!

GOTER: Love.

MOTER: Love!

GOTER: Love.

MOTER: Louder, Goter; louder!

GOTER *(A little louder):* Love!

MOTER *(A little louder):* Love!

The Man continues with his work. The music increases in intensity.

GOTER: Love!

MOTER: Love!

GOTER: Love!

MOTER: Shout, Goter; louder!

GOTER *(Not shouting yet):* Love!

MOTER: Louder!

GOTER *(A brief pause. He shouts):* Spirit of God! Spirit of God! *(With a final piercing shout.)* Love!

MOTER: Love! Love!

The Man throws out water to wash up the blood. It splatters both heads. The music rises simultaneously.

MOTER: Shout, Goter, shout! Love! Love! Love!

The music thunders with the climactic echoing of the Trumpets of the Last Judgment. The Man continues his work and Moter shouts stridently, with the music as background.

MOTER: Love! Love! Love! Love!...

THE END

MARCH

ALBERTO ADELLACH

ALBERTO ADELLACH

ALBERTO ADELLACH

Argentina: 1933-1996

Carlos Alberto Creste (the author's real name) began writing for the theatre in the 1960's under the influence of Beckett and Ionesco, and the "Theatre of the Absurd," but with a markedly Argentine focus. His first version of *Homo Dramaticus* was presented in 1963. It was revised in 1968, and became his best known work: a trilogy that includes the play *Marcha* (March), presented in this anthology. It has been translated into a dozen languages and has been presented many times on nearly every continent.

Between 1970 and 1976 Adellach continued to write for the theatre, but also dedicated himself to radio and television; he founded a publishing house for children's books as well. After a military coup in 1976, he was blacklisted and forced into exile. Soon after he arrived in Spain that year, two of his children were kidnapped by a military group in Argentina and held for a week. Adellach subsequently denounced the atrocities of military dictatorships in articles published in Spain, Mexico and the United States. He lived in Mexico from 1981-1984. From there he went to the United States, making it his home until his death, and never again returning to Argentina

His works for the theatre have won numerous prizes, and have been performed in Spanish, Portuguese, English, German, Italian and Polish. In 2004 the Instituto Nacional del Teatro published his complete works in three volumes.

MARCH

CHARACTERS:

1, 2 and 3. They march in place, keeping in formation. 1 becomes 4, 2 becomes 5, 3 becomes 6, and so on. A drumbeat marks their steps.

1: We're getting there.
2: Yes, thank God, we're getting there.
3: We're moving forward, that's all!
2: No, we're getting there.
1: A few steps more, and there will only be a few steps less.
3: And when there are a few steps less, we'll have taken a few steps more. Ha! *(A pause.)*
2: The important thing is that we're getting there.
1: I like to keep going, and to think that it's just over there. And then I see it. And it's great.
3: Where is anything great? Where is anything so great? You get there if you can. You see what you have to see. And you do what you have to do. And that's it!
1: That's what I say! The thing is, that I like it… *(He holds out his arms. A shot rings out from the back of the hall. 1 falls to the ground, then rolls off to one side, into the darkness. Then he gets up, and takes his place behind the other two. He is a new character.)*
3: You see? They're shooting.
2: So what?
3: What do you mean, "so what?" They start to shout and make noise. So the others shoot.
2: *(Shrugs his shoulders.)* They're always shooting.
3: I know they're always shooting! But they don't have to provoke them.
2: Even if they don't provoke them. *(Another shot. 2 falls. He reappears behind the others.)*
3: I know that too. *(A pause.)*
4: They always shoot, and someone always falls.
3: What?
4: I said they always shoot! And someone always falls!

ALBERTO ADELLACH

5: Of course! Somebody has to fall.
3: Why "of course?" And why does somebody have to fall?
5: Because they're shooting. That's the way it is; some shoot, and some fall.
4: What happens to the ones that get there?
5: They turn around and start shooting.
4: Oh, I see.
3: Because they're after them. Because they provoke them. Because they don't know how to march! *(A shot. He falls.)*
4: For whatever reason.
5: Some shoot and some fall.
4: They won't let them get there.
5: No, they won't.
6: Don't they ever let them?
4: Never. *(A shot rings out. He falls.)*
5: You see? They're shooting.
6: Yes, I see. That's bad.
5: They're falling.
6: Someone will have to do something about this.
5: A politician. They're shooting.
6: A leader.
5: They're falling.
6: Some "strong man."
5: They're shooting.
6: An organizer.
5: They're falling.
7: God!
5: They're shooting... falling... shooting! *(A shot. He falls.)*
6: Lately, God's not for anybody.
7: So?
6: Then this.
7: This what?
6: That they're shooting, don't you see? They're killing them. So what do you expect?
7: No one expects anything, as far as I know.
6: Nobody expects anything, but they're killing them. "They don't have to," but they're killing them! "And nobody told them to come," but they're killing them!
8: Why are they killing them?

MARCH

6: Because they're getting closer. *(A shot. He falls.)*

7: That's terrible. Everybody should have an opportunity.

8: That's right, a turn.

7: A chance. *(His tone changes.)* The rules are open, aren't they? All right, then it's fair-play.

8: Fair-play?

7: Fair-play. *(A shot. He falls.)*

8: Nobody has a chance.

9: Don't say that. It's not right.

8: No opportunities. No chances.

9: Nobody should say that.

10: Yes, they should.

9: You shouldn't even think it.

10: People are thinking it!

9: A person shouldn't—can't—think like that.

8: When someone marches, he thinks. When he thinks, he talks. He starts talking, and he falls. *(A shot rings out. He falls.)* Because you think... you fall... *(He rolls off to the side.)*

10: And you don't think anymore.

9: All the better. That way you don't talk. And you don't say stupid, wrong things.

10: I think what I want to think! And I say what I want to! And if I don't say anything, it's because I don't want to! If I wanted to, I'd say something! Why shouldn't I say what I want to? *(A shot. He falls.)*

11: I don't understand it. I just don't understand it. Somebody is going somewhere and he falls along the way. It just can't be. Something is wrong in this clockwork existence. Something has broken down. It makes me sad. May I throw up?

12: Do whatever you want.

11: What did he say?

9: Do what you want. It's not a very good answer, but what are you going to do? You say that, and that's what they tell you.

12: Who told you to come?

9: Nobody. I just came. But I have eyes and I can talk. I have ears and I say what I think. I'm no different from anybody else.

11: I'm no different from anybody else, either. But I can't stand to be sad. Or to feel like throwing up. *(A shot. He falls.)*

12: I can't stand people who defend the weak.

9: You can't stand them, but they're here. They ought to be here, and

they'll keep on being here, in spite of everything.
12: Who? The defenders?
9: The weak. And then the defenders, as a matter of course.
12: Here we don't need to defend anyone. Here we march. And we have to march. There's no time to think about anything else. We have to march, and that's all there is to it. *(A shot. He falls.)*
9: You see? Because he was in a hurry. *(A shot. He falls too.)*
13: I want to ask them… not to shoot anymore… We don't want… to hurt anybody… We're here because we have to be… Our parents and grandparents were here… We're here, and our children will be here… And our children's children… And all the children of all the children… They can't go on shooting forever… If we could, it would have been better never to have started marching at all. We should have stayed put from the beginning. But now it's a mistake… a huge mistake… an enormous mistake… *(A shot. He falls.)*
14: We shouldn't talk.
15: Of course not.
14: We shouldn't talk, not even to say of course not.
15: We shouldn't talk, not even to say we shouldn't talk.
14: Of course not. *(A shot. He falls.)*
15: We have to keep quiet.
16: I had a son who started marching when he was very young. He was brave and headstrong.
15: Ready, willing and able.
16: What?
15: Ready, willing and able. That's what they say.
16: He was quite a boy. All you had to do was take one look at him, and you could see that he was the cream of the crop. One day he was marching along, and bang.
15: Bang?
16: Bang. *(A shot. He falls.)*
15: That boy was the best there is.
17: The best is strength.
15: Courage.
17: Tenacity.
15: Willpower!
17: *(Wildly.)* Happiness! *(A shot. He falls.)*
15: Per-se-ver-ance. *(A shot. He falls too.)*

MARCH

18: The most important thing is to be above all the vulgar things in life. I invite you all to meditate…
19: Quit screwing off, fellow.
18: I invite you all to sit down.
19: This guy's crazy!
18: I invite you all...
20: Can the invitations buddy. We're in no mood to be invited to anything.
18: You have to put yourself above vulgar things, and below ambition!... *(The others grumble, jab him with their elbows, push him.)* You have to put yourself... Hey, aren't you listening to me?... I'm telling you what you have to do with yourselves!... How to act!... So things won't turn out like this!... Always like this!... *(He stops. A shot rings out. He falls.)*
19: *(After a pause.)* Some guys just keep screwing around, don't they.
20: Yeah.
19: Some guys are really a drag. They just don't seem to know... they don't understand the game... And they ask for cards when the cards have been dealt... *(A shot.)* Like me... They've been dealt to me. *(Another shot.)* Really dealt. *(He rolls to one side.)*
20: Some guys don't understand.
21: They day-dream.
20: Some are believers.
21: *(Opening his arms.)* It takes all kinds! *(A shot. He falls.)*
22: Where are they?... The ones that keep falling, where are they?
20: Over there. Can't you see?
22: I want to see their faces!
20: They're rotting away.
22: Their hands!
20: Rotting.
22: Their feet!
20: Rotting. All rotting away. You couldn't look at anything worse.
23: Nobody comes here to look.
20: They come to march.
23: To go on, with all of this, in spite of it all and against it all! *(A shot. He falls.)*
22: Their hands and feet!
20: All rotting away.
21: And their faces! *(A shot.)* Oh! *(He rolls off to the side.)*
20: Rotten. All rotten.

ALBERTO ADELLACH

24: Come on, slack off a little!
20: Completely rotten. *(A shot. He falls.)*
24: *(To the ones who are shooting.)* Ease off, will you?
25: Let us breathe!
24: Try to understand the newcomers!
25: Ease off a little more, just a little more, just a tiny bit… *(A shot.)* Bastards! *(Another shot. He falls.)*
26: They're getting mad! Don't shout: it makes them mad.
24: Or moan, or stamp your feet: it makes them angry.
26: Or think: it makes them irritated.
24: They won't give us an inch!! *(A shot. He falls.)*
27: *(Jumping in.)* What're we doin', hey, what're we doin'?… Don't push, hey!… This is somethin'—it's really somethin'! *(He jumps.)* Put a stop to this, or I'll start smashin' faces!… Bunch of damn idiots!… Why don't ya pick on somebody yer own size? *(A shot. He falls down, fighting those behind him.)*
28: Well done.
26: Well done?
28: Very well done. The best thing to do to these idiots marching with us is to get rid of them all.
26: You think so?
28: How far can you get with this kind of people coming along?
26: I don't know.
28: You have to throw them out, once and for all!… Liquidate them!… Get rid of the damn puke!! *(A shot. He falls.)*
26: That took care of it. *(A shot. He falls too.)* But…
29: Leave us alone, you shitheads!… Leave us alone, you sons of bitches, bastards, screws!… *(A shot. He falls. The game picks up speed.)*
30: Go ahead and shoot!… What difference does it make?… The red dawn still rises in the East!… *(A shot. He falls.)*
31: You'll get yours. From up there…; you'll go to Hell… Hell is coming… from up there… *(A shot. He falls.)*
33: You crazy bastards!… You damned idiots! Let a man live out his life!… You lunatics!…
32: I don't mind. Let them do what they want with me.
33: Lunatics!…
32: Do what you want! *(A shot. He falls.)*
33: A bunch of damned lunatics! *(A shot. He falls.)*
34: Isn't there a sign here? Isn't there something to show the way? Isn't

MARCH

there anything? Then we're marching toward nothing. We are nothing. *(A shot. He falls.)*

35: How can they shoot while there are still birds? How can they shoot while there are clouds? How can they shoot while life lights our every step with beautiful feelings? *(He stops.)* That, gentlemen, is *my* opinion about the situation. *(A shot. He falls.)*

36: That's enough!!

37: *He* said, "That's enough!..." I didn't say anything. As far as I can see, it's just a word. While the thing... Well, really, I think... Everybody has to take responsibility for what he says, right? Without involving your neighbor. Later you have to take the consequences. The consequences, I... *(A sudden change. He gets down on his knees.)* Don't shoot! I didn't say anything!! I'm not marching toward you! I'm going the other way! *(A shot. He shudders.)* I didn't say any-thing. *(The one coming up from behind pushes him out of the way with his foot. He rolls aside.)*

36: *(Mechanically.)* That's enough. *(A shot. He falls, mechanically.*

38, 39 and 40 continue to march in silence.)

38: All right.

39: All right.

38: They've stopped.

39: That's the way it looks: they've stopped.

40: You never know. Sometimes they listen to reason.

39: And... the sermon.

38: What sermon?

40: The example.

38: What example?

39: The force.

38: What force?

39: From everyone... in the healthy desire to go on, to fulfill ourselves, to do those things that are, well, the very salt of life... *(A shot. He falls.)*

40: The salt and pepper! *(A shot. He falls.)*

38: And the cream! And the sugar! *(A shot. He falls.)*

41: And the butter! You bastards. *(A shot. He falls. The pace increases.)*

42: You murderers! You bastards! *(A shot. He falls.)*

43: You sons of bitches! *(A shot. He falls.)*

44: You're full of shit! *(A shot. He falls.)*

45: Your flesh is shit! *(A shot. He falls.)*

46: Your soul is shit! *(A shot. He falls.)*

123

47: You smell of shit! *(A shot. He falls.)*
48: What are you going to do when nobody goes forward? *(Three shots ring out. They all fall. Only the rhythm of the drum is left on the stage. It grows louder for a moment as the light fades to darkness.)*

CURTAIN

THE DEATH OF ALFRED GREY

RODOLFO SANTANA

RODOLFO SANTANA

RODOLFO SANTANA

Venezuela: 1944-2012

Santana began his activity in the theatre with various groups around Caracas at the age of nineteen. In 1968 his play, *La muerte de Alfredo Gris* (The Death of Alfred Grey) won first prize in a competition at the University of Zulia in Venezuela. In 1970 another play, *Barbarroja*, won the Premio Nacional de Teatro. In 1973 he was invited to the University of California at Los Angeles where he presented his play, *Moloch*, with a group of students from the Department of Spanish and Portuguese. Returning to Venezuela the following year he continued writing and directing pieces for the theatre, and also worked on scripts for films and for television. In 1982 Santana was elected president of the Asociación Venezolano de Profesionales del Teatro. Receiving numerous awards for his writings, at the time of his death his works had been presented outside of Venezuela more than one-hundred times, throughout Latin America, in Europe, and in the United States.

Rodolfo Santana revised his works often. The play, *The Death of Alfred Grey*, was first written with an emphasis on themes and devices found in the Theatre of the Absurd. Prisoner 2 had no idea why he had been sentenced to death, and no explanation was ever given. The Guard was extremely polite, and the Girl was seen as rather flighty. In a later revision (presented in this anthology), slight changes have been inserted to give the play a more realistic feel. The Guard here is much more brutal, the Girl becomes a well-defined prostitute, and most of all the depiction of a universe in which nothing is sensible is lost. Prisoner 2 at first does not understand why he is being punished, but then slowly discovers that it is for political reasons, and somehow comes to accept that. Drawing away from the Theatre of the Absurd, we now have a much more realistic world, but one in which a soul is still lost for all the wrong reasons.

THE DEATH OF ALFRED GREY

CHARACTERS:

Prisoner 1: Wearing only blue pants, fitting snugly against his body. Wears a chain around his neck.
Prisoner 2: Dark clothing. Wearing a dirty shirt and a wrinkled tie. His name is Alfred Grey.
Woman: Scantily dressed. Long hair.
Guard: Blue suit and shirt. He wears no necktie. Carries a large pistol in his belt.

Setting:

A jail cell, dark tones. In one of the walls a small window. Stains and writing on the walls. Two stools and a small table.

SCENE I:

A fight is going on in the prison.

PRISONER 1: (Choking PRISONER 2) Rat!... You're a filthy sewer rat!
PRISONER 2: Forgive!... Forgive!... Forgive me!...
PRISONER 1: Forgive you, you squashed cockroach? *(Choking him.)* I'm not God, I'm not even a priest to forgive you.
PRISONER 1 drags PRISONER 2 along the ground.
PRISONER 2: Have pi!... *(Moans.)* Have some pity!
PRISONER 1: There's no pity. Either you learn or you die. *(He grabs the feet of PRISONER 2 and holds him upside down.)* Are you going to do what I tell you to?
PRISONER 2: Yes, yes.
PRISONER 1: *(Shoves his knees into him.)* If you're lying, I'll give you a beating you'll never forget.
PRISONER 2: I'll obey you, I swear!
PRISONER 1: I'll whip your ass and pour salt in the wounds. You'll scream bloody murder!
PRISONER 2: I'll do whatever you say.
A pause.
PRISONER 1: All right. *(He lets loose of him.)* I just want you to be

reasonable. We're friends, right?

PRISONER 2: Whatever you want…

PRISONER 1: We'll never be enemies. Shake! *(He holds out his hand and squeezes PRISONER 2's hand hard. He smiles.)* Brothers to the end: an iron bond… Right, brother?

PRISONER 2: Of course, brother.

PRISONER 1: *(Lets go of his hand.)* Then this is what we'll do: you sleep on the bottom bunk, so the air in the bottom half of the cell is yours. It's all yours!... I sleep on the top bunk, and the air in that part is mine. Okay?

PRISONER 2: Perfect. Perfect.

PRISONER 1: Let's get a couple points clear: first, I don't want anybody stealing my air. What about you?

PRISONER 2: I don't either.

PRISONER 1: It's nothing special. I'm a thief. I steal everything, from a penny to a million, and that includes stealing other guys' women too. *(He laughs.)* Women! That was a good one, wasn't it?

PRISONER 2: Really good!

PRISONER 1: I've done armed robbery. I've raped girls and broken into houses, but I've never… not once!... stolen anybody else's air. You know why?

PRISONER 2: I suppose you must have your reasons…

PRISONER 1: Robbing air is a very serious crime… It's like taking away the life of the person it belongs to. See?

PRISONER 2: Yes, of course…

PRISONER 1: I'm no murderer. I don't think you are either. I'll never breathe your air, and you're not going to breathe mine.

PRISONER 2: You can count on me.

PRISONER 1: I expected nothing less from you.

PRISONER 2: Of course… then I'll have to walk around bent over. But what does that matter?

PRISONER 1: And I'll have to stand straight up. That does matter! But you'll be better off than me. I won't be able to sit down on the floor. Or lie down on the ground and look up at the ceiling and think deep thoughts… Rum, women, rum, women. *(A brief pause.)* Of course, I won't be bent over, but all the same, you'll have a lot of comforts that I won't have.

PRISONER 2: Comforts?

PRISONER 1: Using the toilet without having an accident! You think that's nothing? I'll have to lift the pot up to my bunk. Hit my head on the ceiling. Keep my balance while I pull down my pants and run the risk of turning the pot over and spilling all the shit on my mattress...

PRISONER 2: Uff!

PRISONER 1: Have you ever slept on a mattress with the stink of shit?

PRISONER 2: Never, but... Why?

A pause.

PRISONER 1: What?

PRISONER 2: Nothing, nothing.

A brief pause.

PRISONER 1: Were you going to say something?

PRISONER 2: It wasn't important... No, I've never slept on a mattress that smelled...

PRISONER 1: I can see that you're a man who's refined and delicate... What were you going to say to me?

PRISONER 2: It was just foolishness.

PRISONER 1: *(Pounces on him and begins to beat him.)* Keeping secrets, are you? What were you going to say, you dirty dog?

PRISONER 2: It was nonsense.

PRISONER 1: *(Using his legs, he gets PRISONER 2's neck in a scissors grip and chokes him.)* You're going to come crystal clear even if I have to squeeze the nonsense out of you.

PRISONER 2: Let go of me!

PRISONER 1: Talk!

PRISONER 2: *(Moaning.)* I thought we could share the air without marking out areas that are yours or mine. We would be more comfortable, and we wouldn't infringe on each other's rights by accident – which could happen at any time.

PRISONER 1: *(Lets him loose. A pause.)* Impossible. It would be a violation of the rules of lung hygiene.

PRISONER 2: I don't understand.

PRISONER 1: (He sits back down on PRISONER 2, and tries out wrestling holds on him.) You don't have to understand. Just take my word for it. *(A brief pause.)* It's not healthy to breathe someone else's air. It's immoral. *(He twists PRISONER 2's arm. PRISONER 2 cries out.)* No complaining: you stay in your air, and I'll stay in mine.

PRISONER 2: Whatever you say! Anything you say!

PRISONER 2 gets up and takes a few steps, bent over.

PRISONER 1: You ought to be glad. No one else's lungs are going to contaminate your air.
PRISONER 2: Of course. That' right. How stupid of me…
PRISONER 1: Are you satisfied?
PRISONER 2: Yes, very… *(He walks around.)* Tell me…
PRISONER 1: What?
PRISONER 2: Could I, once in a while…, just for the heck of it, you know…, stand up straight, next to the window, and get a little sun?
PRISONER 1: Sorry, but no, my friend. The sunlight that comes through that window is mine. I have a right to it, see? And I have to protect my rights.
PRISONER 2: What about the sunlight that hits the floor?
PRISONER 1: Ah, that's different! Sure, you can have that!
PRISONER 2: Thank you.
PRISONER 1: But still, I can get between you and that sunlight whenever I want to, in the upper part of the cell that belongs to me.

Sunlight comes in through the window opening. It strikes the floor. PRISONER 2 walks over to it and basks in the light. PRISONER 1 goes over and puts himself between the sun's rays and PRISONER 2.

PRISONER 2: Could you move a little?
PRISONER 1: No.
PRISONER 2: Just for a minute or two. Just for a few seconds, that's all. It won't hurt you.
PRISONER 1: I like to feel the warmth of the sun.
PRISONER 2: That's not fair, and you know it!
PRISONER 1: I'm within my rights.
PRISONER 2: It's not fair!
PRISONER 1: You don't think so? Maybe if I pound on you a little, you'll change your mind. *(Jumps on him and begins to beat him.)* Take that, you little shit!
PRISONER 2: Don't hit me!
PRISONER 1: Am I fair or not?
PRISONER 2: Very fair… Very…
PRISONER 1: Now that's what I like. Now you're being reasonable. *(A brief pause.)* What's happening is you're not satisfied with what you've got. You're ambitious, and I'm not… Look at me: right now I'd really like to sit down on the floor, but I won't, because I'd be taking away your rights, and to me they're sacred.
PRISONER 2: I wouldn't mind if you sat on the floor. Not at all! I'd

be very glad if you did.

PRISONER 1: *(He goes over to PRISONER 2 and shakes him.)* Stand up for your rights, you little coward. You've got to stand up for them. You need to be strong and tough about what's yours, and defend it like a cornered tiger.

PRISONER 2: All right! All right! I understand.

PRISONER 1: *(Lets go of him. A brief pause.)* Would you be mad if I laid down on the floor of the cell?

PRISONER 2: *(A brief pause.)* Why…, yes. Very mad.

PRISONER 1: Why?

PRISONER 2: You would be infringing on my rights… The floor is part of my territory and… and nobody's ass is going to dirty it except my own.

PRISONER 1: Very good! And just what would you do if somebody did spit on your rights? What if they breathed your air or laid down on your floor?

PRISONER 2: Don't mess around with me: I'd strangle him!

PRISONER 1: Excellent!

PRISONER 2: I'd spit in his face! I'd stomp him!

PRISONER 1: That's what I like to hear!

PRISONER 2: You shit-head, I'd tell him. You're a son of a bitch!

PRISONER 1: Perfect!... So you really know what you have and what you want?

PRISONER 2: That's right, and I'm not going to let…

PRISONER 1 sits down on the floor.

PRISONER 2: *(Watching PRISONER 1. Startled.)* What are you doing?

PRISONER 1: What did you say?

PRISONER 2: Uhh…, you're…

PRISONER 1: Sitting on the floor here.

PRISONER 2: Infringing on what belongs to me!

PRISONER 1: Nice and comfy.

PRISONER 2: My rights!... It was your idea… the top part is yours. The top part!

PRISONER 1: So?

PRISONER 2: You're in the bottom part, in my part… You're breaking… Get up!

A pause.

PRISONER 1: I'm not going to get up.

A pause.

PRISONER 2: I give you my permission to sit down.
PRISONER 1: I am sitting down... without your permission. I don't need it.
PRISONER 2: *(Smiles.)* You joker!
PRISONER 1 smiles. PRISONER 2 bursts out laughing.
PRISONER 2: I knew it was a joke all along.
PRISONER 1 laughs out loud. PRISONER 2 stands up straight, happy. PRISONER 1 jumps on him and chokes him for a few minutes.
PRISONER 1: It's no joke, you fucking asshole! If you're not going to protect your rights, I'm going to defend mine!... You breathed my air, you goddam cockroach!
PRISONER 1 throws PRISONER 2 to the ground.
PRISONER 2: You sat on my floor! You took my air... You took what belongs to me!
PRISONER 1: You won't defend it, so it belongs to whoever wants it. Just dare to touch what's mine, and you'll see what happens. Next time, I'll kill you.

SCENE II

A Guard enters, with a Woman.

GUARD: Good afternoon, assholes.
PRISONER 1: *(Grabbing hold of the bars.)* What a good looking dame you've got with you, Mister Guard.
GUARD: This woman is my lover.
PRISONER 1: *(To the Woman)* Charmed, Gorgeous.
GUARD: I came here on official business, and I decided to bring her along.
PRISONER 1: What a set of knockers!
GUARD: She's always wanted to see some real live prisoners in their cells.
WOMAN: The poor little things!
GUARD: She thinks it's so romantic!
WOMAN: They're like caged animals.
GUARD: The official business I have is...
PRISONER 1: *(To the Woman.)* Look at that waistline! Turn around so I can see your ass, would you?

THE DEATH OF ALFRED GREY

WOMAN: How exciting! It reminds me of when my Daddy used to take me to the zoo.

GUARD: *(To PRISONER 2.)* I'm here to inform you, my little pigeon, that by order of the judge and jury...

PRISONER 1: What hips. Lift up your dress so I can see your legs, will you?...

GUARD: Filthy people in our society, basing their judgments on the sacred laws of their rotten conscience...

PRISONER 1: What a dish! What a doll!

WOMAN: They look like little monkeys. *(She laughs. To PRISONER 1.)* Here, monkey, monkey...

GUARD: Wanting to preserve the shit we live in from those germs that are doing everything they can to destroy it...

WOMAN: Want a peanut?

PRISONER 1: *(Touching his genitals)* How about you? Want to see my pud?

PRISONER 1 laughs and the Woman flirts with him.

GUARD: You have been given the death penalty.

PRISONER 2: What? Me? The death penalty?

PRISONER 1: *(To the Woman)* I bet you're dynamite in bed, baby. Hey guard, am I right?

GUARD: More or less.

WOMAN: *(To the Guard.)* If I had any peanuts I'd give them some. Bread crumbs or bananas... They're so sweet...

GUARD: If you want to appeal, do it through your lawyer. *(He laughs.)* Lawyers!

PRISONER 1: Guard! If I give you a dime, will you let me hump the girl?

GUARD: A dime?

PRISONER 2: But I haven't committed any crime!

WOMAN: *(To the Guard.)* What does he think I am, a piece of scum?

GUARD: You don't think that's enough?

WOMAN: Hell, no!

PRISONER 1: Fifteen cents!

WOMAN: More than that.

GUARD: Can't you pay more?

PRISONER 2: What are they accusing me of?

PRISONER 1: Fifteen cents is all I got.

The Woman shakes her head.

GUARD: I'm sorry. It's not enough.
PRISONER 2: What sentence or judge or lawyer are you talking about?
GUARD: Nobody. But you're going to be shot anyway.
PRISONER 1: *(To the Woman.)* Come on, sweetie. I'll give you all the money I got. It will only take a minute, and I haven't had a woman for five months. It will just be a quickie.
WOMAN: *(Shaking her head.)* I haven't sunk that low.
GUARD: She says she won't, you pig. You'll just have to jack-off.
PRISONER 2: *(To the Guard.)* Listen to me!
Guard looks at PRISONER 2.
PRISONER 1: *(To the Woman.)* Look, baby… Come here.
GUARD: Ah, you again!… What do you want?
PRISONER 2: It's a joke, isn't it? That business about shooting me?
PRISONER 1: *(To the Woman.)* Why are you being so hard-nosed?
GUARD: It's no joke. You'll face a firing squad, and you'll have an honor guard taking you to the wall. Isn't that good enough for you? *(To the Woman.)* Let's go, cunt.
PRISONER 1: Hey, guard, bring her back in a week. I think I can get a little more money by then…
WOMAN: *(To the Prisoners.)* Goodbye, boys. I'm going to tell everybody about this experience. I bet they won't believe me when I tell them about the expressions on your faces.
PRISONER 2: There has to be some mistake!
GUARD: Good afternoon, you slimy slugs.
Woman and Guard start to go out.
PRISONER 1: Sweetie. Sweetie pie! Baby! Don't leave me like this!
PRISONER 2: I protest! I haven't committed any crime!
The Guard and the Woman leave. PRISONER 2 moans.
PRISONER 1: You're killing me, ass!
A pause.

SCENE III

PRISONER 1: *(To PRISONER 2.)* Did you like that woman? *(As though he has heard a reply.)* Sure! How could you help but like her? *(A pause.)* Those solid bazongas. That round ass. Firm legs. *(He grunts like an animal.)* That's what I call a real woman!… The guard's lover. His woman! I bet he doesn't satisfy her: that guard is a cold fish. He's pulled out the fingernails of too many men. He's castrated so many of them that he hasn't got any feelings anymore. Did you get a look at his mouth? A tiny thing, cruel. The mouth of an impotent sadist. Don't you think?... Sure! What that woman needs is a man like me: bad, hard... Who'll hump her three times in the morning, once before lunch, two times for an afternoon snack and five times at night. *(He roars.)* That's me! *(He looks at PRISONER 2 who is moaning, clinging to the bars.)* What's the matter with you? *(A brief pause.)* Got a headache?

PRISONER 2: No.

PRISONER 1: That dame make your balls ache?

PRISONER 2. No. No.

PRISONER 1: You want some of the sunshine coming through the window?

PRISONER 2: No!

PRISONER 1: *(Shouts.)* You want to breathe my air?

PRISONER 2: Not that either?

PRISONER 1: So what is it then? Sniveling is what women and fags and little kids do. When a man jerks out a tear, it ought to be because he's really hurting. Did the guard tell you something?

PRISONER 2: Yes!... That's it!... It's incredible... It can't be right... It's all a mistake!

PRISONER 1: Calm down. What's so unbelievable? What kind of mistake?

PRISONER 2: They gave me the death penalty.

PRISONER 1: What? What?

PRISONER 2: Tomorrow, at sunrise, I'll face a firing squad.

PRISONER 1: I don't believe it.

PRISONER 2: The guard told me so... We had a long talk.

PRISONER 1: *(Pensive.)* A little shrimp like you. *(Nervously.)* I don't know... *(Incredulous.)* How could they have given you death?... I mean... Huh! Who would ever have thought it?...

PRISONER 2: Thought what?

PRISONER 1: *(Pensive.)* Huh?... Oh, nothing... I was just talking to myself... *(A pause.)* So! You've been making a fool of me!

PRISONER 2: *(Attempting to ward off any blows by hiding his face in his arms.)* No! No!

PRISONER 1: *(Laughing nervously.)* What a joker! *(He keeps up his nervous little laugh.)* Jo-ker!... I always knew you were lying... I knew it from the start. You're a real ragger!... Nobody could be such a coward...,

especially someone who's been sentenced to die…
PRISONER 2: But you…?
PRISONER 1: You were just playing along, right, friend? *(He laughs and claps PRISONER 2 on the back.)* These jails get so boring if you don't find some way to pass the time.
PRISONER 2: I'm no joker! *(He faces PRISONER 1 while stooped over.)* All the while I've been in this cell I've had no time for joking. What do you think? That this is a vacation for me? And now, with the news that they're going to execute me… Do you think I'm in any mood for making jokes?
PRISONER 1: Sorry. *(Somewhat respectfully.)* Yeah, I suppose you're serious all right.
PRISONER 2: I am being serious! *(He stands up straight, and then quickly bends back down.)* Your air!... I didn't mean…
PRISONER 1: I don't care… *(He gives a false laugh.)* What a terrific cellmate you are! *(He laughs.)* But now, if we were being serious about it, I'd be more than happy to mix my germs with yours.
He laughs. PRISONER 2 looks at him, disconcerted by the evident change in his relationship with his cellmate. A pause.
PRISONER 2: What's wrong?
PRISONER 1: With me? Nothing.
PRISONER 2: Are you afraid of me?
PRISONER 1: I've never been afraid of anyone or anything in my entire life!
PRISONER 2: *(Moving toward PRISONER 1.)* Are you sure?
PRISONER 1: *(Stepping back.)* I'm sure! I'm sure!
PRISONER 2: *(Hurls himself at PRISONER 1, and shakes him.)* You're afraid of me, you filthy swine! You jellyfish!
PRISONER 1: I respect you.
PRISONER 2: You respect me? *(Shakes him.)* This isn't another one of your dirty little games?
PRISONER 1: No, no way! *(He extricates himself from the grasp of PRISONER 2.)* I'm an enemy of weak people, a friend of the strong ones. *(A pause.)* I think we're all like that…, don't you? The opposite of a hero. Someone who's been given a death sentence is dangerous, no two ways about it… You can count on him as being one of the strong.
PRISONER 2: I'm no criminal. I can't be sentenced to die. The guard made a mistake. So did the judge and the jury. The law is wrong,

and in this case justice isn't worth the paper it's written on... I'm innocent, innocent of any crime!

PRISONER 1: Law? Justice? *(He laughs.)* What a joker! Don't come to me with fairy-tales!

PRISONER 2: So, what can a person trust then?

PRISONER 1: Look, you don't have to be so cagey with me. I'm not going to ask you about the crime you committed.

PRISONER 2: I'm not guilty of anything!

PRISONER 1: All right, all right... *(A brief pause.)* Of course, I would like to know...

PRISONER 2: I'm going to sit down. By tonight this whole mess will be straightened out. The guard will come, and he'll tell me it was all a mistake.

PRISONER 1: I think we ought to be honest with each other. Don't you?

PRISONER 2: Yes. Of course.

PRISONER 1: A friendly relationship. We're like brothers, aren't we?

PRISONER 2: Yes, yes.

PRISONER 1: Can I breathe your air?

PRISONER 2: You said it was all a joke.

PRISONER 1: Just so there won't be any misunderstandings. Can I breathe it?

PRISONER 2: I don't care.

PRISONER 1: Thanks. *(He bends over.)* What was the crime you committed?

PRISONER 2: There wasn't any.

PRISONER 1: What do you mean?

PRISONER 2: I have no idea what crime they're accusing me of.

PRISONER 1: You don't know which one of your jobs won you the grand prize?

PRISONER 2: Listen to me. In this case, men and justice have gone off on some incomprehensible path. A harsh sentence has been passed down based on an absolutely absurd reason, since it doesn't exist.

PRISONER 1: To tell you the truth, I don't understand a word you're saying.

PRISONER 2: Pay attention... It's as though I were a snake, and suddenly I found myself surrounded by a group of falcons that were getting ready to tear me apart for no reason at all.

PRISONER 1: A snake! So you're a snake and you've been sentenced to death for no reason! Ha!

PRISONER 2: I'm not a snake. That was just an example. I could just as well have said I'm a dove.

PRISONER 1: *(Laughing.)* A dove? You?

PRISONER 2: A balloon. Yes, a balloon!... With a bunch of little boys around it who decide to burst it after a long discussion... and maybe laughing about it.

PRISONER 1: You're the biggest damn liar I've come across in my entire life. *(A brief pause.)* You're like Osvaldo do Santos – inside, I mean. He was black as midnight and as evil as a scorpion. He's dead now. By this time he's probably thrown out Lucifer and taken over his place in hell. *(Looking closely at PRISONER 2.)* Yeah, you're like him.

PRISONER 2: Please, don't think I'm such a... twisted... kind of person.

PRISONER 1: Did you murder somebody?

PRISONER 2: What?... But... are you serious? Everything I said to you...

PRISONER 1: *(Rather impatient.)* Come on, come on... Was it a rape? Did you kidnap some little kids or something?

PRISONER 2: I like children! *(A pause.)* I could never hurt them... I don't earn much money in my job at the bank, but I always bought caramel candy and gave it to the little children whenever I had a chance.

PRISONER 1: A bank? Now I get it! You killed the manager, and robbed the bank and ran off with the secretary. It made a real splash: I read about it in the newspapers a few months back.

PRISONER 2: How many times do I have to tell you? I'm innocent! I couldn't possibly steal a penny or kill anyone. And especially not Mr. Mendoza: he was always so nice to me.

PRISONER 1: Mr. Mendoza?

PRISONER 2: The bank manager... Once he invited me to his house for dinner. It was after I had been working for him for twenty years. I met his wife and his daughter. *(He laughs while thinking about it.)* The meal was delicious: turkey, burgundy wine, a cheese soufflé.

PRISONER 1: Okay! Are we through beating around the bush? Are you going to tell me why they sent you up?

PRISONER 2: Don't get upset...

THE DEATH OF ALFRED GREY

PRISONER 1: Damn, but you make my blood boil...! I can see why you're proud of what got you the death sentence, and that you want to keep quiet about it. But you're wrong about not telling me, your cellmate. The only person who's going to be with you in your final hours!

PRISONER 2: I didn't mean to upset you, but the truth is... even though you think otherwise, I'm really...

SCENE IV

The Guard enters.

GUARD: How's our future corpse doing?

PRISONER 2: *(Grabbing hold of the bars.)* Thank God! I thought it was all going to turn out as badly as I imagined it might! *(A brief pause.)* So?... Has everything been straightened out?

GUARD: Of course, you little dead man. We don't make many mistakes in this prison...

PRISONER 2: Thank goodness... *(He gives a sigh of relief.)* You don't know how grateful I am to you... *(To PRISONER 1.)* You see? *(To the Guard.)* For a little while I was afraid something might go wrong.

GUARD: I feel like giving you a good pounding. How could you ever imagine that we keep bungling things up time after time.

PRISONER 2: I'm sorry...

GUARD: The car has been arranged for now... We didn't have one, but then we thought of the ambulance.

PRISONER 2: What about it?

GUARD: We'll take you to a deserted place in the ambulance. We've already picked out the spot. It's in a very pretty grove of pine trees outside the city limits.

PRISONER 2: What are you saying? What?...

GUARD: Me and Fatty Moncho are going to be the ones that'll shoot you. You know, while trying to escape and all those other wild risks you take. And we'll riddle your ass full of bullets.

PRISONER 2: You're crazy!

GUARD: The Minister of the Interior turned down your petition for a pardon. He's the one who's crazy.

PRISONER 2: I never even submitted a petition to be pardoned. There's been a terrible mistake here!

GUARD: I'm sorry. If you have some complaint, you need to tell God in heaven about it. I only know that I'm going to load my sawed off shotgun full of dum dum bullets.

PRISONER 2: Who can I talk to? I want to explain my problem to someone else... Anyone but you!

GUARD: Careful, little one. You don't want to be smart with me, or I'll cut out your tongue. *(He takes out a few cigarettes.)* Take one, it's marijuana... Fatty Moncho sends it to you, so you won't say we're treating you bad.

PRISONER 2: Marijuana? Fatty Moncho?

GUARD: Fatty Moncho is the warden of this prison.

PRISONER 2: The warden?

GUARD: The biggest pisser of them all.

PRISONER 2: He's giving me marijuana?

GUARD: That's right.

PRISONER 2: *(Embarrassed.)* Thank you. *(He slowly takes the marijuana cigarette.)* I didn't think the warden even knew I existed.

GUARD: He likes you. And besides, he doesn't like to see people cry. He sent you the marijuana to make you real happy!

PRISONER 2: When they brought me to this place, beating and kicking me, I tried to talk the warden...

GUARD: Call him "Fatty." He likes that.

PRISONER 2: To Fatty. But they wouldn't let me. I was able to see the door to his office – big, with green glass and a large sign over the transom... Then I fainted, and I woke up here... *(To the Guard.)* Tell Fatty Moncho that I'm grateful for what he's done.

GUARD: He'll be touched. He likes guys who are macho. Do you need anything else?

PRISONER 2: No, nothing.

GUARD: I'll leave then... I'll come back later with a little food.

The Guard turns and goes out.

SCENE IV

PRISONER 1: Damn, but you're lucky! Even Fatty Moncho respects you.

PRISONER 2: Fatty Moncho is very kind.

PRISONER 1: I... I respect you too. You've been given the death sentence, and still you keep your cool.. I've never met anybody with balls like you.

PRISONER 2: *(Flattered.)* Come on, don't fool around...

PRISONER 1: I'm not fooling! *(He crosses himself.)* I swear on my mother's grave!

PRISONER 2: You're kind. Even though I'm not... Well, I have been given the death sentence, but I didn't commit any crime.

PRISONER 1: *(Laughs.)* What a stubborn mule!... Look, we're brothers, aren't we?

PRISONER 2: Yes, yes.

PRISONER 1: We share everything. We breathe the same air. Our piss gets mixed in the same toilet bowl, and still you don't trust me.

PRISONER 2: I didn't mean to be impolite, but... Don't you see?

PRISONER 1: *(Animatedly.)* Are you going to tell me what crime you committed or not? It must have been a real humdinger the way you're keeping quiet about it. Something awesome that I can tell my grandkids about, if I ever have any.

PRISONER 2 laughs, pleased.

PRISONER 2: You're a sly one.

PRISONER 1: Come on, tell me.

PRISONER 2: All right. Here's what happened. *(He thinks.)* When was it?... Wednesday..., yes, Wednesday. I was walking along the avenue and a skinny yellow dog was running around in front of me. The sun had just gone down and the streetlights were already lit up. In the window of a building there were several flower pots with geraniums, and in front of one house a fat man with a moustache, wearing a tee-shirt and smoking a cigarette was watering a dried up pine tree in his yard. *(A brief pause.)* I don't think that tree will ever come back to life, but the fat man didn't seem to be concerned with the laws of nature, and he kept watering it very conscientiously... Farther up the street I saw a lot of people running... Yes, it was a demonstration... They were throwing posters and signs down on the ground, and they were running... And at that moment it all happened...

A pause, PRISONER 1 licks his lips in anticipation.

PRISONER 1: Go on! What happened then?

PRISONER 2: A car stopped right next to me. Two men got out and started shooting at the people. They killed several of them... I could see the whole massacre... Yes, I saw it... Then the men started beating on me with their batons, kicking me, swearing, and spitting on me. And they threw me into their car and brought me here... That's all.

PRISONER 1: But... What about the crime?

PRISONER 2: Well, there was the massacre of all the people in the demonstration...

PRISONER 1: I mean the crime you committed... Did you kill the fat man and hack off his moustache? Did you go up to the apartment with the geraniums and kill the woman after you raped her? Something! Something dirty, rotten, despicable?

PRISONER 2: No, nothing of the sort. It all happened the way I just got through telling you...

PRISONER 1: I don't believe you!

PRISONER 2: That's what happened!

PRISONER 1: No!

PRISONER 2: Yes!

PRISONER 1: That's a bunch of shit!... Or... could it be... that you're just a little bank clerk, and you're letting them execute you without putting up a word of protest?

PRISONER 2: I am protesting!

PRISONER 1: A stupid, innocent little jerk? A pig who's not worthy of being in this cell with me? *(He approaches him in a menacing manner.)* Is that what you are?

PRISONER 2: Hold it! Hold it! *(A brief pause.)* Don't get so hot under the collar... I don't know... I respect you... You know? You're like a brother to me... Fatty Moncho is a good person too... And the guard... It's just that, well... the massacre, but... Maybe... Yes, it must be... It's quite possible that I did commit a crime.

PRISONER 1: Finally, you're coming clean... Thanks... I was afraid...

PRISONER 2: *(Concentrating.)* Some crime. But what? I must have committed one. Yes... That's the only possible explanation for everything that's happened... *(To PRISONER 1.)* Maybe...

PRISONER 1: No maybes, if you don't mind.

PRISONER 2: You're right. *(A brief pause.)* What must have happened is that I went out of my head for a minute... I killed the fat man with the moustache, and then I went up the apartment and raped the woman and then killed her.

PRISONER 1: They can't sentence a man to death if he commits a crime while he's not in his right mind. You must have been absolutely aware of what you were doing, since they've given you the death penalty.

A pause.

PRISONER 2: You're right *(To himself.)* Is he right?... Yes, yes.

PRISONER 1: You killed the fat man, then: you're really a wild one!... And you raped the woman. You've got balls!

He bends over and kisses the hands of PRISONER 2.

PRISONER 2: What are you doing?

PRISONER 1: Showing you much I really admire you.

He looks at him with near adoration in his eyes. Suddenly he takes out a match and strikes it. Then he puts it next to the marijuana cigarette that PRISONER 2 has in his hands.

PRISONER 2: *(Without thinking, he lifts the cigarette to his lips and lights it.)* Thanks...

PRISONER 1: I'll never forget this time here. *(PRISONER 2 smokes.)* Every word you say will be Gospel to me. I'm going to copy you, my friend... *(A pause.)* Did the fat man suffer much?

PRISONER 2: Well, no... *(Looks at the cigarette.)* Marijuana... *(He laughs.)* When I hit someone, it's always in exactly the right spot. No shit! One blow, and it's certain death... it's inevitable. *(He laughs.)* The fat man didn't suffer, and the woman... *(A short pause. He laughs.)* She enjoyed every minute of it! A real hotty! *(He laughs.)* There was fear in her eyes, but she kept moving her hips like a cement mixer.

PRISONER 1: *(Laughs.)* That's the way they all are!

PRISONER 2: I jumped over the rail into the garden, and jabbed the fat man in the neck.

PRISONER 1: Did you take his money?

PRISONER 2: *(Instinctively.)* No! No! *(A pause. He laughs.)* Well... yes. It was so I could rob him. Of course!... I took his watch, a chain, two rings, his shoes – they were high-class shoes...

PRISONER 1: *(Laughs.)* What about the woman? What did she look like?

PRISONER 2: Ahh!... *(He laughs.)*... A blonde... Blonde?... Wide hips, long legs... A beauty! *(He laughs.)* A real beauty!

Loud laughter that gradually diminishes. PRISONER 2 feels ill. He hands the marijuana cigarette to PRISONER 1 who puts it away. He watches his cellmate who goes over to where the toilet bowl is and vomits. He goes over to help him.

PRISONER 1: Are you feeling sick?

PRISONER 2: Yes. Really sick.

PRISONER 1: You look pale. I'm going to call the guard. You can't die here, in this shitty way.

PRISONER 2: No. No. Don't do anything... It's the air... it feels so heavy.

PRISONER 1: Yes. It does.

PRISONER 2: I don't like this cell. Or any jail cell. This is the first time I've ever been in jail.

PRISONER 1: Didn't they ever catch you before?

PRISONER 2: *(A short pause.)* No, never... *(He goes over to the window opening and breathes deeply.)* It's a lovely afternoon out there...

PRISONER 1: What would you be doing if you weren't in here?

PRISONER 2: Well... Walking around the park with my children... Attacking the people passing by... Visiting some friend... Blackmailing the lovers!... *(A short pause.)* Having a cold glass of beer... Kidnapping a kid for ransom and then killing him!

He cries out and drops to the ground.

PRISONER 1: What's wrong with you, tough guy? Are you going soft on me now?

PRISONER 2: Don't you see? Huh? *(He shouts.)* Can't you understand me?

PRISONER 1: What's to understand? What is it?

PRISONER 2: Is this me?

PRISONER 1: What are you saying?

PRISONER 2: Can this be happening to someone who is completely normal, who has a minimum of pleasures, vices and virtues? A man who was never violent, and who never thought violence would reach out and touch him? Can this really be happening?

PRISONER 1: I don't understand you, my brother.

PRISONER 2: Of course you don't. You're still walking on your tightrope. Your cord hasn't broken. *(A pause. To himself.)* I am Alfred Grey... I am Alfred Grey... I am Alfred Grey... Nothing has happened. Life has gone along as usual. I've followed all the rules. I've been a good citizen. I've never said a word about anything. I've never raised my hand. I've never cried out. I never protested against any massacres. I brought my family up according to religious teachings... I am Alfred Grey... Marijuana? Did I ever

THE DEATH OF ALFRED GREY

think, in all my life, that I'd be smoking marijuana?

SCENE VI

GUARD: Good evening, you dirty bastard sons-of-bitches.

PRISONER 2: *(Going over to the window grate.)* Yes, it is evening now.

GUARD: It's a dark night. It's raining up north.

PRISONER 2: You can't see it from here.

GUARD: Of course not, stupid. That window faces south.

PRISONER 1: *(Pointing to the tray.)* What's that, Guard?

GUARD: This is the dinner for our prisoner who's going to be executed.

PRISONER 2: What dinner?

The Guard sets the tray on one of the wooden stools, and removes the cloth.

GUARD: Ah, doesn't that look delicious? We want you to be fat and satisfied right up to your last minute. Full stomach, happy heart!

PRISONER 2: It all looks… very good.

PRISONER 1: Terrific! What a lucky guy you are!

PRISONER 2: It looks delicious.

GUARD: And it tastes even better. This is the best way we know of to show that we treat our citizens in a top notch way. Even misfits like you.

PRISONER 2: I've never said that you treat anyone badly. *(To PRISONER 1.)* Did I?

PRISONER 1: Never.

PRISONER 2: I never criticize…

GUARD: That's all right. Go ahead and eat.

PRISONER 2: Me, for example, I can't complain. *(To PRISONER 1)* Did I ever complain? *(PRISONER 1 shakes his head.)* *(To the Guard.)* You see? I'm no trouble-maker.

GUARD: Your dinner's getting cold.

PRISONER 2: *(Smiles timidly.)* I'm… I'm terribly hungry.

GUARD: Eat, then. You'll like it.

PRISONER 1: And who wouldn't? A meal like that!

GUARD: I envy you, you cockroach.

PRISONER 1: So do I…, cockroach…

PRISONER 2: Thank you.

A pause. The Guard and PRISONER 1 watch Alfred Grey eat.

GUARD: There was a lot of shooting and killing where they picked you up. Did you notice?

PRISONER 2: *(Thinks.)* No. *(A brief pause.)* This chicken is delicious.

PRISONER 1: And the wine?

PRISONER 2: Out of this world! Would you like a little?

PRISONER 1: No, no. It's all yours, it belongs to you.

GUARD: We don't have any right to any of that great dinner of yours.

PRISONER 2: Oh, please! Just one glass!

GUARD: Certainly not!

PRISONER 2: Are we friends, or aren't we?

PRISONER 1: Of course we are, but friendship means you have to have consideration and respect.

GUARD: And all those nice things that you deserve.

PRISONER 2: As a favor to me… Just one glass,… please.

A brief pause.

PRISONER 1: Just one!

GUARD: All right, but only because you're insisting way too much.

PRISONER 2: I know.

Alfred Grey offers a glass to the Guard, and then another to PRISONER 1.

GUARD: Delicious.

PRISONER 1: Ahh! It's been a long time since my gullet's had this kind of pleasure…

PRISONER 2: I've never tasted a wine this good either.

GUARD: It's really strange that you didn't see any dead bodies when we picked you up. It was a tremendous slaughter. The streets were full of books and workers' helmets. I can't understand how someone like you could get mixed up in such a mess.

PRISONER 2: I wasn't involved in it. Would you like a little chicken?

PRISONER 1: No, thanks.

PRISONER 2: *(Laughs.)* I guess I'll eat it all myself then.

GUARD: It was an ugly affair. We need to justify certain things, and you'll be very useful to us…

PRISONER 1: *(To the Guard.)* What condition was the woman in when they found her, Guard?

GUARD: Shot twice in the back. She tried to run… There were a lot like her.

PRISONER 1: And raped too! *(He slaps PRISONER 2 on the back.)* You're a real terror.

GUARD: They found the terrorists' plans in your pocket. Names. Dates. Meeting places. Codes…

THE DEATH OF ALFRED GREY

PRISONER 2: On me? Are they crazy?
GUARD: Pure lies. It was all made up, of course. But it will help us.
PRISONER 2: Good Lord! I've never tasted anything this delicious!
GUARD: *(Laughs.)* I like you. I'll tell Fatty Moncho you enjoyed your meal. You know? He's taken a real interest in you; of course, you're critical to us.
PRISONER 2: I feel very honored.
PRISONER 1: The death penalty has its advantages, my friend... They pamper you. They respect you. A good meal, and you don't have to be afraid death will come on you unexpectedly.
PRISONER 2: You're right. *(He wipes his mouth with the napkin.)* I'm very satisfied. The dinner was delicious.
GUARD: Can I take away the tray?
PRISONER 2: Whenever you like. *(To PRISONER 1.)* Unless you would like the leftover wine.
PRISONER 1: Delighted! *(He lifts the bottle and takes a long swig.)* Ahh!
GUARD: *(To PRISONER 2.)* Do you have any money?
PRISONER 2: A little... Why?
GUARD: Give it to me, and I'll bring you a surprise. *(PRISONER 2 searches in his pockets and hands his money to the Guard.)*
PRISONER 1: To those who are condemned to die! *(He gulps down the rest of the bottle.)* To your health!
PRISONER 2: What's the surprise?
GUARD: If I tell you, it won't be a surprise.
PRISONER 2: That doesn't matter. Tell me what it is.
GUARD: Take it easy, my little lamb. You'll see, in a little while.

SCENE VII

PRISONER 2: *(To the Guard, through the bars.)* Tell me something. Just a hint. *(Discouraged.)* He left... There's going to be a surprise for me. Another one. *(A brief pause.)* I wonder what it is.
A pause. He goes over to the window bars.
PRISONER 1: Is it light out there?
PRISONER 2: It's all electric lights. The sky is dark.
PRISONER 1: Are there a lot of bright lights?
PRISONER 2: Not many. There are two... No, three neon lights that are bright. One is blinking red. *(A pause.)* Like an explosion in the dark... It says, "Great Circus of the South." "Wonderful attractions

and games." "Everyone loses or wins."

PRISONER 1: The Circus of the South is very interesting. Lions that are faggots. Elephants that dance the can-can…

PRISONER 2: I've never been to it. "Everyone loses or wins." Why? Anyone has a right not to gamble.

PRISONER 1: Not at the Circus of the South. When you go in, you're already gambling.

PRISONER 2: I wouldn't gamble.

PRISONER 1: Then you wouldn't be able to get into the Circus. You'd never see the huge pile of elephant shit. There's enough of it to cover a whole family, including their cat.

PRISONER 2: Have you gone there a lot?

PRISONER 1: Yeah. Once or twice I tried to rob the ticket window. That was the biggest attraction for me… A big, juicy, tempting ticket window.

PRISONER 2: *(Observing PRISONER 1 closely.)* You know, you're really a nice guy.

PRISONER 1: Huh? *(A pause. He laughs.)* Yeah, sure. That's what all the whores tell me.

PRISONER 2: I'm no whore. *(He laughs. PRISONER 1 laughs too.)* You're different from the prisoner I knew this morning. Remember?

PRISONER 1: I didn't know you'd been given the death sentence!

A pause.

PRISONER 2: Neither did I. Now we both know it, and we've both changed.

SCENE VII

The Woman enters.

PRISONER 1: *(Shouts.)* Look who's here! *(He grabs hold of the bars.)* Angel! You're torturing me!

WOMAN: Hello, hello.

PRISONER 1: Sweetie!… Come closer!… That's right, up to the bars. We can do it standing up!

WOMAN: Are you the one they're going to execute?

PRISONER 1: What?… No. *(Pointing to PRISONER 2)* He is.

THE DEATH OF ALFRED GREY

WOMAN: Hello, my lovely boy. What are you doing over there, next to the window? Star-gazing?

PRISONER 2: The sky is dark.

WOMAN: I came… The guard gave me your money. I didn't want to…, you know? But he told me you were all alone and that you were going to be executed, so I came right away. Come over here.

PRISONER 2 doesn't move.

WOMAN: Then I'll go in. *(She opens the door to the cell and goes inside.)* Anything, to be near you, as the lovers say. *(She goes up to PRISONER 2, embracing him and kissing him passionately.)* Do you want me to be your love?… Your girlfriend?… Your girlfriend for tonight?

PRISONER 2: I… well…

PRISONER 1: *(Whispering.)* Yes. Yes.

PRISONER 2: Yes.

WOMAN: Love at first sight, how beautiful! *(She embraces PRISONER 2 and leads him over to the cot.)* I don't want you to die, you seem so nice! I'm going to make you happy. Okay? When they shoot you in the back tomorrow, you'll remember me.

PRISONER 2: Yes, I'll remember you.

PRISONER 1: Lay down on the bunk and spread your legs!

They sit down on the lower part of the bunk bed.

WOMAN: What do you want me to be? Your mother, your sister, your girlfriend, your lover, or just a whore?

PRISONER 1: Your whore! Your whore!

PRISONER 2: Well… the truth is… I…

WOMAN: Do you like me?

PRISONER 1: Yes, yes! A lot!

PRISONER 2: Very much…

WOMAN: How wonderful!

The Woman presses herself against PRISONER 2's chest.

PRISONER 1: *(To PRISONER 2.)* Tell her to take off her clothes and lay down! Have her take them off so she's naked! Squeeze her tits!

WOMAN: I'll remember every one of the bricks in this cell… your face… The girls in the whorehouse will turn green with envy when I tell them about my tragedy.

PRISONER 2: Take off your…

WOMAN: They're not going to believe me. That's why I brought along a camera, so I can capture all the drama of this evening. *(She takes it out of her purse.)* See?

PRISONER 2: Your dress… lie down… take off your…

WOMAN: *(To PRISONER 1.)* Would you mind taking our picture?

PRISONER 1: Anything you want, doll.

PRISONER 1 takes the camera. He stands back. The Woman strikes a dramatic pose next to PRISONER 2.

PRISONER 1: That's it. It's going to be a great photograph, beautiful. That's for sure.

WOMAN: Very kind of you. Maybe one of these days… *(She takes the camera from PRISONER 1)* …we can talk, you and I.

PRISONER 1: I'll give you all I got.

WOMAN: *(To PRISONER 2.)* The girls at the whorehouse aren't going to call me a liar now. And I'm going to ask Fatty Moncho for a signed paper to prove that I stayed with a death row prisoner on his last night.

PRISONER 1: *(To PRISONER 2.)* Tell her to get in the bed! To take off her clothes!

WOMAN: *(To PRISONER 2.)* Kiss me! *(She pushes him down on the bed. She caresses his face.)* You poor thing, tomorrow they're going to kill you. Awful, isn't it?

PRISONER 2: Yes… awful.

WOMAN: Here I am, next to you.

PRISONER 1: Turn her over! Hug her! Bite her!

PRISONER 2: You are… You… yes…

WOMAN: I'll always think of you. I'll be faithful to you.

PRISONER 2: I know.

WOMAN: Our love won't be torn apart by any cruel death.

PRISONER 1: *(Desperate.)* Do it! Get on top of her! Dig in your heels and go to it!

WOMAN: I'll remember this last kiss. The last one I'll ever give. *(She kisses him on the forehead.)* Goodbye. *(She gets up and leaves quickly. A pause. The Woman comes back.)* I forgot my purse!

The Woman picks up her purse. She leaves.

SCENE IX

A pause.

PRISONER 1: What a woman! *(A pause.)* And she really loves you… I think she was crying when she left… She must have gone to the whorehouse, to forget for a while. *(He goes over to PRISONER 2.)* What a lucky guy you are! You had someone to keep you company in your final hours. Other guys aren't so lucky. Me, for instance... It's been years since I had a woman...

PRISONER 2: There's not much time left... Is there?

PRISONER 1: No. The time has really gone by fast. How are you feeling now?

PRISONER 2: I can't explain it... I've never felt like this before. *(A brief pause.)* She left...

PRISONER 1: She was crying. She was losing it.

PRISONER 2: Something else, along with all the rest of this... In my balloon-like existence, surrounded by little kids, ready to burst me apart... And my wife?... My children?... My friends?

A tapping noise comes from the walls. Sharp sounds, in code.

PRISONER 2: What's that noise?

PRISONER 1: Someone's trying to tell us something. *(PRISONER 1 puts his ear next to the wall and deciphers the message.)* It's the other prisoners in the jail. *(A pause.)* We, the prisoners in this jail... *(A short pause.)* We want to offer you... *(More tapping.)* our most sincere respect... *(A pause.)* For being a terrorist... an agitator of society... *(A brief pause.)* From the Association of Prisoners... "Light Fingers Lucho... President..." What do you say?

PRISONER 2: Give them my thanks. My heartfelt thanks. My regards to them all.

PRISONER 1 taps on the wall for a few moments. More tapping comes back. PRISONER 1 listens.

PRISONER 1: It's them again... *(A brief pause.)* They say that there's a priest who's been arrested, and he's in this jail if you need some spiritual help. *(A brief pause.)*... The priest says that he can give you genuine comfort because he's a convict too.

PRISONER 2: I don't have anything to confess. *(He thinks.)* Or better yet... tell him about my crimes... Yes. About what I did to the fat man and the woman.

PRISONER 1 taps on the wall. More tapping comes back.

PRISONER 1: He says you're a devil... *(A brief pause.)* "Ego te absolvo... in the name of the Father, the Son, and the Holy Spirit..." You've been forgiven..., at least by God.

PRISONER 2: Thank you...

PRISONER 1: Are you afraid?

PRISONER 2: Not very... I feel strange, like I'm not me.
PRISONER 1: Go take a leak, that will help you relax.
PRISONER 2: I will. *(PRISONER 2 goes to the back of the stage and picks up the pot. With his back to the audience he simulates urinating. He comes back.)* You were right. That relieves the tension.
Noises. Screams from someone being tortured.
PRISONER 1: Another day is starting. They shouldn't be long now.
PRISONER 2: Yes. What should I do?
PRISONER 1: I don't know... You're the brave one. If it was me, I'd be whimpering like a little dog. I'll never forget you.
Footsteps are heard. Someone gives orders.
PRISONER 2: It's all coming to an end... It's like there's a new tightrope under my feet... *(He walks.)* A different kind of cord... A false note... My life... false... *(To PRISONER 1)* How can I know if that's right? Tell me.
PRISONER 1: I don't know.
PRISONER 2: Why? Tell me! Tell me!
PRISONER 2 shakes PRISONER 1.
PRISONER 1: I don't know!
PRISONER 2: You fucker, tell me or I'll kill you!
PRISONER 1: How can you ask me to tell you something that I don't understand?
PRISONER 2: I'll kill you!

SCENE X

The Guard enters.

GUARD: Aha! The animal inside you is making its appearance. You poor little dead boy! You'd better calm down. Else you're going to get a real beating.
PRISONER 2: You've all been playing with me the whole time... You cockroach. Dead boy. Terrorist. I'm not going to be anybody's little wimp. You understand?
GUARD: Are we playing games? *(He takes out a pistol and goes into the cell.)* This is very serious, my dear little corpse.
A pause.
PRISONER 2: Yes... it looks that way.
GUARD: Shall we go?

THE DEATH OF ALFRED GREY

PRISONER 2: Yes. *(To PRISONER 1.)* Goodbye, fool. My friend.
PRISONER 1: Goodbye, dear friend.
PRISONER 2: I leave you my air, and all the whores you want.
PRISONER 1: Thank you.
GUARD: Try to be on your best behavior. Fatty Moncho thinks you're a great person.
PRISONER 2: I'll try not to disappoint him. I'll do whatever you say.
GUARD: *(To PRISONER 1.)* She'll take fifteen cents.
PRISONER 1: Are you sure?
GUARD: She'll be here shortly. You can't kiss her on the mouth or squeeze her tits. Treat her nice.
PRISONER 1: Don't worry. You won't get any complaints.
GUARD: *(To PRISONER 2.)* Let's go.

SCENE XI

PRISONER 1 watches them through the bars.
PRISONER 1: So long… *(A brief pause.)* What a lucky guy!
PRISONER 1 goes over to the bunk bed and straightens out the sheet. He takes a comb out of his pocket and runs it through his hair. He sits down on the bunk. He takes out the marijuana cigarette, lights it and inhales deeply.
PRISONER 1: Now, we wait for the whore to get here.

END

THE CRUCIFIXION

CARLOS SOLÓRZANO

CARLOS SOLÓRZASNO

CARLOS SOLÓRZANO FERNÁNDEZ

Guatemala – Mexico: 1919-2011

Considered one of the most important playwrights in Guatemalan history, Carlos Solórzano moved to Mexico in 1939, and later became a citizen of that country. He graduated from the Universidad Nacional Autónoma de México where he studied architecture and literature. In 1948 he received a grant from the Rockefeller Foundation that allowed him to study drama at the Sorbonne. There he met several men who would influence his later writings, including Albert Camus and Michel de Ghelderode. He was a professor and theatre director at several universities in Latin America and the United States.

From 1953 to 1960 he took part in the theatrical group, Teatro Universitario, which presented works by Christopher Fry, Albert Camus and Eugene Ionesco, among others. Many of Solórzano's own works have been translated into English, French, German Russian and Italian, and have been performed throughout Europe and the Western Hemisphere. In addition to his plays, he was a journalist and wrote novels and scholarly works. *El crucificado* (The Crucifixion) of this anthology was penned in 1957.

When asked why some of his works are iconoclastic, he responded: "Because I wished to topple some idols that dull the minds of our people: the Church hierarchy, the military, those so-called democratic structures that are ways of using the popular vote so that those who are in control can become wealthy and nothing will change."

THE CRUCIFIXION

CHARACTERS:

Jesus (A 30-year-old man of the village. Weak. A feverish look, Indian characteristics.)
Mary (Mother of Jesus. An old lady of the village.)
Magdalene (A girl of the village, dark, robust.)
Four men who play the parts of the four Disciples.
The Priest.
Men and women of the village.

The action takes place on Good Friday in a small Mexican village where each year at this time the Passion of Christ is performed.

Setting:

The interior of a hut: smoke-stained walls, a dirt floor. In the corner a small fire used for cooking. Downstage, left, a small door that leads to the other room in the hut. At the rear a double door standing open, allowing us to see the blue fields blending with the sky.

Two men and two women of the village, dressed in Mexican fashion, are on stage, arranging various objects. We see a tunic of purple satin lying over a chair. On the table is a crown of thorns. A large cross of rough wood rests against one wall.

Scene One

1ST MAN: Well, everything is ready.
2ND MAN *(Happily)*: Yes, everything. I was the one who put those two pieces of wood together for the cross. *(He runs his hand over it fondly.)* It is nice, don't you think?
1ST WOMAN: I sewed the purple tunic.
2ND WOMAN: I wove the crown of thorns together—and I had to be careful not to prick my hands.

Jesus enters from the left, his head down. He is dressed in peasant clothing, but he already has on the wig of flowing hair and the beard to resemble Christ.

1ST WOMAN: Hello, Jesus. You must be happy!

JESUS *(Quietly)*: Yes.

1ST MAN: Anybody would think that you're sad. You haven't even tried on your tunic…

JESUS: There is still time.

1ST WOMAN: Only a few minutes. It won't be long till they will be coming for you. What's wrong? You look as though you have a fever.

JESUS *(Absently)*: I hadn't noticed.

2ND WOMAN: That's not so surprising. After all, they are going to crucify him. *(She bursts out laughing, but her laughter breaks off when she looks at Jesus.)*

JESUS *(Intensely)*: Yes, they are going to crucify me.

2ND WOMAN: You are lucky. The Priest chose you and your family to be in the crucifixion scene because he says that you look like the real Jesus. After this is over, everyone in the village is going to respect you. Now that I think of it, the men in your mother's family have always played the role of Christ. Do you remember your grandfather? His name was Jesus too. *(Superstitiously.)* He died a few days after he played the part. *(With a forced laugh.)* Quite a coincidence, wasn't it?

JESUS: Be quiet.

1ST WOMAN: What's the matter with you?

JESUS *(Timidly)*: I'm afraid to die.

1ST MAN: Christ was afraid to die too. That's why it was so sad.

2ND MAN: But they are not going to kill you.

JESUS: But what if they have to?

2ND MAN: Have to?

JESUS: Yes. So that they can be saved.

1ST MAN: Be saved? From what?

JESUS: The Priest says that they have to be saved from something.

1ST MAN: No one has ever been saved from anything by killing a man. Calm down.

2ND MAN: The Priest says that a sacrifice is the only way they can be forgiven for their sins. Especially for original sin.

1ST MAN: What's that?

2ND MAN: I don't know. I think it is a way of saying that it's sad to have been born and to have to die.

THE CRUCIFIXION

JESUS: No, it means that we have sinned just by being born.

1ST MAN: Well, what... I didn't sin. I was born and that's all. I didn't even ask to be born. Look at us, stuck out here on this land where there are no trees, where the sun dries up a man's insides and turns him into a pile of ashes. *(A distant shouting is heard.)*

JESUS *(Alarmed):* They are coming for me. They're coming because they want me to be sacrificed.

1ST MAN: They aren't going to do anything to you. They will only whip you a few times, nothing else...

1ST WOMAN: The lashes from that whip will make everyone respect you afterwards.

2ND WOMAN: And you will be able to enter the kingdom of heaven because of them.

JESUS: But what if they crucify me?

2ND WOMAN: Don't say dumb things like that.

JESUS *(Not listening):* If they crucify me... When the cross is so close, it is almost a temptation!

1ST MAN: But we are just going to have some fun for a while. Sometimes people need these celebrations: you pray a little, and you get drunk a little at the same time. You are going to have fun too. You'll see. You won't even feel the weight of the cross when you are drunk and you carry it through all those shouting people.

2ND MAN: That's right. Besides, there is no reason for you to be afraid. You aren't the real Savior. You are only a man like all the rest of us.

1ST WOMAN: He is just caught up in his role.

1ST MAN: What role?

2ND WOMAN: Of a man who is going to be crucified.

1ST MAN *(Laughing out loud):* Oh, what a Messiah we have here... You're not going to start believing that nonsense about going to a sacrifice... You're going to a party. We are all going to a party, a celebration. Aren't we?

JESUS *(As he looks at the door at rear, he steps back):* Here they come...

Four men of the village, with marked Indian features, appear in the doorway; they are dressed in the usual clothing of the Passion Play: lustrine garments with gilt trim. Underneath the tunics which are too short for them, we see their pants and their old shoes. The wigs lie askew on their heads, and their cloaks are only partly fastened.

1ST WOMAN *(With a note of dread):* The Disciples!

CARLOS SOLÓRZASNO

A DISCIPLE: Where is that Messiah?
PETER: Where is Jesus?
1ST WOMAN *(To the 2nd Woman)*: He's Saint Peter.
PETER: Where is the Master?
JESUS *(Theatrically)*: Here I am. *(The Disciples kneel before him. One of them falls over and rolls on the floor while the others laugh.)*
PETER: Help him up.
1ST WOMAN: The one who fell down is Saint Matthew.
JESUS: What's wrong with him?
PETER: He's drunk.
MATTHEW *(Getting up)*: We're all drunk.
PETER: Yes. We are all drunk. And you are going to get drunk too, Jesus.
JESUS: No. I know that when people get too drunk there is always a crucifixion.
MATTHEW *(Offering him a bottle)*: Have a drink. Come on, take a drink. Or aren't you a man?
JOHN *(Intervening)*: Show them that you are just as much a man as they are.
MARK: Even more of a man. More than a man.
MATTHEW: Take a drink, Jesus. Go on, have a drink. If a man doesn't get drunk there is nothing worth living for. Not even a sacrifice. Isn't that right? *(He laughs and wipes off his drunken slaver.)*
He holds the bottle out to Jesus. Jesus takes it, hesitates. Everyone is watching him. Suddenly, with a decisive gesture, he puts the bottle to his lips and takes a long drink... He wipes off his mouth, and assumes a pose of solemnity; he climbs up on the table, and standing there he speaks with a theatrical air.
JESUS: Love ye one another!
MATTHEW: What did he say?
Mark struggles with Peter to get hold of the bottle.
MARK: Give me that bottle.
JESUS: I said: Love ye one another!
MATTHEW *(Looking at him bewildered)*: Why?
JESUS: Because it is good.
MATTHEW: Who says so?
JESUS: I do.
MATTHEW: And who are you? A poor imitation of the Messiah, that's what. You don't think we are going to take you seriously, do you? *(He turns his back on him.)*

THE CRUCIFIXION

JESUS: Listen to me...

MATTHEW *(Drinking):* I'll listen to you when you are good and drunk, just to keep from getting bored. *(He hands him the bottle again.)* Have another drink. *(Jesus hesitates.)* Tell him to take another drink. If he doesn't, he will never be able to bear up under the cross, or from the shouts of those people who will be waiting for him out there, or from the beatings with the whip. Nobody can take all that unless he is drunk.

PETER *(Seeing the anguished expression on Jesus' face):* Don't be afraid. After this is all over you will be sort of a miracle to everyone; they will take pictures of you, they will light candles to you...

JESUS: But what if they hurt me? What if they kill me?

PETER *(Laughing):* Well, you will still have one consolation: the resurrection!

JESUS *(Hesitating):* The resurrection... Give me a drink. *(He drinks once more. The liquor spills out of his mouth and runs down the sides of the bottle. He tries to stand up, but he is giddy. He falls into a chair and sits there.)*

1ST WOMAN *(To the 2nd Woman):* Now! Put his tunic and his crown on him now. *(The two women approach Jesus, and with no resistance on his part they pull the tunic down over his head and tie it at the waist. Then they place the crown of thorns on his head and straighten his wig. In the shadows the illusion will be perfect. He will look like a statue of Christ from any rural church: very dark, his eyes shining, both hands hanging loosely at his sides. When they see him the two women kneel before him. The light from the fire, rear, lends an unreal glow.)*

1ST WOMAN *(Kneeling):* Our Father which art in heaven, hallowed be Thy name. Give us this day our daily bread...

2ND WOMAN: Forgive us our debts as we forgive our debtors...

Their praying trails off

JESUS: What are these women doing?

PETER *(Very cautiously):* They are praying to you.

JESUS *(Astonished):* Already? But they haven't crucified me yet. *(Meditating.)* Or... am I really the Savior?

MATTHEW *(Giving him a hard clap on the back that makes him pitch forward):* Yes, Jesus. Yes. You are the Savior. Take another drink and you will feel like the son of all the gods on earth. *(Jesus takes the bottle, drinks, and stands up violently, causing the kneeling women to fall over on the ground.)*

JESUS *(With the glow of inebriation in his eyes):* I am the son of God.

MATTHEW *(Laughing out loud):* That's right. They say that we are all sons of God, but if you insist, you are more a son of God than we are.

JESUS *(Continuing, drunkenly):* And even though I am afraid, it is written that I must die for them. *(He points his finger around at the others.)*

MATTHEW: We all have to die, but it isn't for something. *(He drinks some more.)*

PETER: Enough. No more drinking. We are not even going to know what we are doing. And Jesus won't be able to carry the cross.

MATTHEW: We will help him with the cross. Now and forever. If he isn't drunk, no one is going to believe anything. And what is most important is that the actors should believe too. *(The Disciples drink, Jesus drinks, the men drink. The women look at them without comprehending.)*

1ST WOMAN: Jesus. Your mother is here.

2ND WOMAN: Mary, Mary. I am so glad you have come. Do something to make them stop.

Mary appears in the doorway. She is old and hulky. She is wearing the tunic and cloak of the Virgin. On her head she has a "halo" that seems constantly about to fall off.

MARY: What is going on?

1ST WOMAN: They're drunk. They are all drunk.

MARY: Jesus too?

1ST WOMAN: He is the worst one of all. He keeps saying very strange things.

MARY *(To Jesus):* Son...

JESUS: Woman. *(He points to John.)* Behold thy son...

MARY *(Indignant):* Are you so drunk that you don't recognize your own mother?

JESUS: I have no mother. Only a father. Yes; I do have a father. *(He looks up.)*

1ST WOMAN: Of all the disrespectful...

MARY: You really should not talk about your father: you don't even know who he was.

Everyone laughs loudly.

JESUS *(Not listening):* It is written. The son of man will shed his blood to wash away the sins of the world.

MARY *(Shaking him hard):* Son, come to your senses. Don't say such wild things.

JESUS *(Drunk):* You remember that there was only one loaf of bread

THE CRUCIFIXION

here? Now there are many. *(Triumphant.)* My power has made them multiply.

MARY: But I bought those loaves of bread myself, this morning.

JESUS: You don't believe me? Oh, woman of little faith. *(To the Disciples.)* Is it not true that I gave sight to a blind man, that I made the dumb speak? *(He raises his fist menacingly.)* Is it not true? *(Peter signals to the others to go along with Jesus' drunken ranting.)*

PETER *(Wearily)*: Yes, Jesus, yes.

JESUS: And that I brought the dead back to life?

DISCIPLES *(Complacently)*: Well... Yes.

JESUS: And that I must sacrifice myself for everyone?

MATTHEW: Yes, yes. Don't get all upset now.

JESUS *(Transfigured)*: Love ye one another!

MARY: What is going on, son? Tomorrow you have to be well and sound so that you can do the planting. I will need you. After being drunk like this you could get sick. I don't like to see you drunk. *(She takes off the halo.)* The best thing would be for you to tell everyone to go away and that we won't put on the Passion Play.

JESUS: Do you want to turn me away from my mission for such a small thing as planting the fields?

MARY: What are you talking about? The fields are what we make our living from. What would we do without them? You, with all your words and crazy talk, couldn't feed us if no one did the planting. Wake up. Remember, you are just a poor boy, the son of a lone woman who has to make a living every day.

JESUS: Store up for yourself treasures in heaven.

MARY: You won't get us any food with that sort of talk! Will you?!

1ST WOMAN: That's right. Scold him. Men always like to think they're more than they really are.

JESUS *(Theatrically)*: I am the truth and the life.

MARY: No. What you are is a lunatic who wants to solve everything with words. *(Suddenly tender.)* Calm down, son. Why don't you eat something to make you sober up?

Magdalene appears in the doorway. She is wearing her hair loose, and her clothing too is appropriate for the Passion Play. Her clothes cling to her body, letting us see her round, full, appetizing figure clearly.

MAGDALENE: You mother is right, Jesus.

JESUS: Magdalene, dear Magdalene. *(He embraces her, then he backs off.)* What am I doing? This is a sin.

MAGDALENE: You are drunk! We might as well not have the Passion Play at all! With you like this...

MATTHEW: You are wrong, Magdalene. It is only with Jesus drunk that we will be able to go through with this to the end.

JESUS *(Ecstatic)*: It is written. I must die so that I can rise from the dead.

MARY *(To Magdalene)*: I'm afraid. You are going to be his wife—you tell him not to go out in that condition. Listen to those people outside. They are drunk too. *(Offstage we hear the shouting of the people celebrating Holy Week.)*

MAGDALENE: Jesus, don't go out there like that. I am afraid of all this drunkenness. Yours, and the people out there too.

JESUS: It is written that I must go.

MAGDALENE: Written? Where?

JESUS *(Perplexed)*: Well... I don't know, but it is written.

MAGDALENE: Don't go out. Just think, what if something should happen to you now that I am going to be your wife? *(She draws close.)* That's all you should be thinking about now. You and me, together.... Life is really going to begin now.

JESUS: Life will begin when I die and come back from the dead.

MAGDALENE: Stop talking like that. If you and I are going to live together...

JESUS *(Interrupting)*: That doesn't matter.

MAGDALENE: What do you mean? That is the only thing that does matter. *(The Priest appears in the doorway. He comes in with obvious signs of satisfaction.)*

PRIEST: Is everything ready? The people are wildly enthusiastic. They want to see Jesus.

MAGDALENE: Jesus is not going. *(She closes the door.)*

PRIEST: Open the door. He has to go.

MARY *(In anguish)*: Why?

PRIEST: For the people to believe, they have to see him.

MARY: Listen to them shouting. They will hurt him.

PRIEST: This is only a play.

MARY: But they could kill him.

PRIEST: Nobody dies at a celebration.

MARY: What about the other Jesus? His grandfather?

PRIEST: Open the door, I said. It's his duty to go. He will play his role well.

THE CRUCIFIXION

MARY: And those people outside? Won't they forget that he is just playing a role?

PRIEST: They will see him, and they'll believe.

MARY: In what?

PRIEST: In what they need to believe.

MARY: I don't understand.

PRIEST: It isn't necessary to understand. Just to believe. Now let's go. *(He motions to the Disciples.)* The Disciples, here on the right, in a line. Mary, Saint John, and you, Magdalene, back here. And you get ready, Jesus; it's time to take up the cross. *(Everyone obeys, laughing and joking.)*

JESUS *(Trying to lift the cross)*: I can't. It is too heavy.

As the laughter continues, the Priest faces them all, very severely.

PRIEST: Quiet. Starting right now I don't want to hear any more laughing. *(Everyone quiets down. The Priest opens the door and we hear loud shouting.)*

PRIEST *(To Jesus)*: When this is over I'm going to give you a silver cross as an award.

MARY *(Making a final attempt)*: What if he doesn't go, father?

PRIEST: Everyone would stop believing in Jesus.

MARY: In which Jesus? This one here?

MAGDALENE: I believe in this Jesus. I believe in him. *(She tries to embrace him but Jesus pushes her away.)*

PRIEST: Let's go, I said.

Jesus, his eyes shining with drunkenness, places himself under the cross which two men of the village are holding up. He drinks for the last time with satisfaction, then he straightens up, supporting the cross by himself.

JESUS: I am the Savior. It will be a glorious day. It is as though something is just beginning... *(He hiccoughs involuntarily. Then he laughs with empty, foolish, mindless laughter.)*

MAGDALENE: I hope it's not just the opposite: that something is going to end.

The Priest begins to direct the procession. The Disciples begin moving. Behind them goes Jesus, stumbling. Then Mary, Magdalene, and Saint John. As the procession goes out an intense shouting explodes outside the hut, then the noise of firecrackers, shrill whistles and applause, all combined with the music of a small local band playing a lachrymose, discordant tune. At the end of the procession goes the Priest, dispensing his blessing. The light slowly dims until there is absolute DARKNESS.

CARLOS SOLÓRZASNO

Scene Two

When the light comes on again, the Disciples are on stage. It is dark. An occasional last shout or the sad burst of a distant firecracker is heard. The Disciples have removed their wigs. Only one or two are wearing beards; another has pulled up his tunic, revealing his patched and dirty pants.)

PETER: I just can't believe it.

MATTHEW: What will we do now?

JOHN: It was not our fault. If those drunks really crucified Jesus it was only because he was drunk too and he kept shouting at them: "I am the Savior. Nail me up. Nail me up."

PETER: I don't remember anything. I was dead drunk. *(To John.)* But you could have stopped it.

JOHN: I tried to, but they wouldn't let me. While one man was whipping Jesus, he kept shouting at them, "Hit me harder, harder," and then another man came, and another one, and pretty soon they were all whipping him. When I saw that they were really going to nail him up, I yelled at them to stop; but they were all shouting so loud, and the Priest had already gone to the church, and Jesus was frantic and he kept saying to them, over and over: "It is written, kill me, kill me." Afterward, all I could do was take him a last drink when he was already nailed up, but he kept repeating like a madman: "I thirst, I thirst…"

PETER: We were all thirsty. Because we were drunk. Why don't you say something, Mark?

MARK *(Pensive):* Something is going to happen. They are going to blame us. We all got him drunk here and sent him out to be sacrificed. Matthew was the worst. He kept telling him: "You are the Savior, You are the Savior," over and over, all afternoon long.

MATTHEW: I don't remember anything.

JOHN: I don't either.

MARK: But that poor bastard believed it, and he died.

JOHN: No one will ever know who killed him. We all killed him, but nobody killed him. No one is guilty.

PETER: But Mark is right. They will blame us. Especially Matthew, Mark, and John—his best friends.

THE CRUCIFIXION

MARK: He was really to blame himself. As soon as the procession went out of here he started shouting and stamping his feet, just begging to be sacrificed. When you ask people to kill you, it does no good to complain afterward.

JOHN: But this Jesus was different.

MARK: Different?

JOHN: Yes. There was something special about him that the rest of us don't have.

MARK: Huh! You are only saying that because they crucified him. If it had not been for that… he would be just like everyone else.

JOHN: Don't you think it was because he had a little of the spirit of the Savior in him?

MATTHEW: What are you talking about?

JOHN: I have listened to the Priest. That can happen; the spirit of the Savior…

MATTHEW *(Snapping his fingers)*: I have an idea.

JOHN: What?

MATTHEW: We will say that it was a miracle. That Jesus was a kind of Savior, and that he had to die.

MARK: Not a bad idea. Then the authorities would not be able to blame us for anything.

PETER *(Beaming)*: It's a good idea!

MATTHEW: And what if they don't believe us?

PETER: There are four of us. And if four men start repeating the same thing, over and over again, they will all end up believing us. *(He winks at them.)*

MARK: That's true. Let us swear right here and now that Jesus was the Savior.

The four men hold out their hands, putting them one on top of the other.

DISCIPLES *(Chanting.)*: Jesus was the Savior, Jesus was the Savior, Jesus was the Savior.

JOHN: There is one more thing… If they ask us: "The savior of what?" what do we tell them?

PETER: I don't know. Anything. That doesn't matter. We will look up at the sky without answering, that's all.

MATTHEW: All right. Now we need to get away from here. The authorities are going to investigate, and we will have to go into hiding. And someday maybe something will come from all this… You never know…

JOHN: I don't understand.
MATTHEW: Yes, something worthwhile…
JOHN: For who?
MATTHEW: For us, of course. For us.
PETER: Let's go now, and don't forget. *(He signals to them. The Disciples repeat the chant once more.)*
DISCIPLES: Jesus was the Savior.
(They nod to each other, and after looking carefully at the entrance, they all go out in different directions. When the Disciples leave, Mary and Magdalene appear in the small doorway on the left. They are no longer wearing the costumes of the Passion Play, and their clothing looks very dirty and shabby.

Scene Three

Mary leans on Magdalene's arm and cries silently, unable to speak.

MAGDALENE: Go on: cry. There's nothing else you can do. But he was the real cause of it all. He walked out there, going from drunkenness to his death without knowing it, and he left us here alone, poor, hungry, forgotten. *(She stifles a sob, then reacts angrily.)* The poor man probably thought that by his death we would gain something… *(Mary hides her face in Magdalene's bosom. Magdalene strokes Mary's head with pained compassion while, very slowly, the curtain falls.)*

THE END

THE EVE OF THE EXECUTION
OR GENESIS WAS TOMORROW

JORGE DÍAZ

JORGE DÍAZ

JORGE DÍAZ GUTIÉRREZ

Argentina-Chile: 1930-2007

Born in Argentina, Jorge Díaz lived in Chile (where he eventually became a citizen) from the age of three until he was thirty-five years old. He studied architecture at the Universidad Católica de Chile. In 1959 he joined the theatrical group, Ictus, working as a set designer, actor, director and dramatist. This group presented plays by Eugene Ionesco, among others, that would influence his later writings. In 1961 he wrote and presented one of his most famous works, *El cepillo de dientes* (The Toothbrush), an ironical illustration of the lack of communication between people.

Writing over one-hundred works for the theatre (although often classified under the denomination "Theatre of the Absurd," he preferred to call them "grotesque theatre"), Díaz also penned scripts for radio and television, and wrote short stories. His works have garnered many awards, including the Premio Palencia de Teatro (Spain) and the Premio Antonio Buero Vallejo. They have also been translated into many languages and have been presented on stages worldwide.

In 1965 Díaz left Chile for Spain, where he wrote under the censorship of the Franco regime. That same year he penned *La víspera del degüello o El génesis fue mañana* (The Eve of the Execution or Genesis Was Tomorrow, included in this anthology), with its apocalyptic vision of the end of mankind. During his years in Spain, he formed a children's theatre group, Los Trabalenguas (The Tongue-Twisters). In 1994 he returned to Chile.

Of himself, Jorge Díaz once said, "I am not a writer. Without a group behind me, I cannot write one line. I am an architect who sees words in space."

THE EVE OF THE EXECUTION

And the evening and the morning were the first day.

(Genesis, I, 5)

CHARACTERS:

Louse
Guardian
Hosanna

This work can be presented wherever there are no obstacles. As the lights are dimmed and the room is left in darkness, there is a great silence. Children's innocent laughter rings out, possibly to the accompaniment of stringed instruments. Then in the darkness there is a dull, far away sound of a terrible explosion that lingers, vibrating in the air, as though in emptiness, full of echoes and strange sounds.

The explosion has cut short the laughter. The explosion could be accompanied by a sudden flash of light that illuminates the stage for an instant, and then plunges it again into darkness. Then, very slowly, a weak light begins to illuminate the stage.

A dirty, barefoot girl, her hair completely disheveled, enters: her expression is one of primitive innocence. She is wearing nondescript, ragged clothing which completely covers the shape of her body, and comes falling down to her feet.

One foot is bare, the other is wrapped in an old rag. Actually she is nothing but a formless hulk of dirty old rags, with only her face showing— which is that of a young animal with quick reflexes.

Her movements are brusque, and show a general lack of coordination common to certain types of mental retardation. She grunts and makes other incoherent noises. Once in a long while she will laugh. But her eyes are always attentive and thoughtful. She should communicate to the audience a kind of profound and instinctive worry which borders on the terrifying, the kind one experiences when observing some inexplicable natural phenomenon.

She enters and sits down, her legs apart; she simply slumps to the ground, and stares at the palm of her left hand, emitting guttural noises. Almost immediately voices are heard offstage.

JORGE DÍAZ

GUARDIAN'S VOICE: What have you done with yourself?

HOSANNA'S VOICE *(Laughing):* The poor thing thinks it's all over.

GUARDIAN'S VOICE: Come here, stupid!... This is just the beginning, it's not the end of anything.

HOSANNA'S VOICE: I get tired of looking at her.

GUARDIAN'S VOICE: You don't have to look at her, dear. Just let her push you.

The voices continue, but their words or the meaning of their words fade or become blurred. The crazy girl— that's what we'll call her for the moment, even though we're not exactly sure what she is—has risen instinctively, and she goes offstage for a moment. She comes back carrying pieces of metal. They should be large pieces of rusty metal the origin of which it would be impossible to say. They might be remnants of a great catastrophe, or simply the outgrowths of a highly advanced civilization. The general appearance of the metal that the crazy girl keeps piling up in the rear is mysterious and terrible, and at times as ordinary as a garbage can. The horizontal lighting will accentuate the sharp edges and corners of the rusty metal.

The crazy girl has by now brought in a large quantity of metal, and she has disappeared once more, continually emitting guttural sounds that might at some point be reminiscent of a chant.

Almost immediately Hosanna and Guardian appear. They are very old. Hosanna has on a rumpled wedding dress with strips of cloth hanging down which she straightens and arranges from time to time, involuntarily, like a "tic, "an action which has been repeated over and over again for years.

Her face has been powdered and pathetically painted with cosmetics.

In one hand she still holds a withered bouquet of flowers. In the other she has a metal cane. She limps.

Guardian is wearing formal striped trousers and a black dinner jacket. The elbows and collar are somewhat greasy, and he has a withered carnation in the buttonhole. They are both rather dusty, and they maintain a dignity that is not the slightest bit ridiculous, but which may be somewhat disconcerting.

Guardian is pushing a rickety child's cart, like a junk collector uses.

In fact, inside the cart we can see an assortment of odd, unexpected utensils, along with the edges of a rather dirty sheet and pillow. Guardian and Hosanna talk animatedly, but they do not appear disturbed or excited by what they say. A sort of routine dialogue, a mutual agreement of nonhostility, floats between them, broken at times by sudden explosions of restrained violence. As they enter they

THE EVE OF THE EXECUTION

are in the middle of a conversation.
HOSANNA: Were they copulating, Guardian?
GUARDIAN: They were copulating, Hosanna.
HOSANNA: Right there...?
GUARDIAN: There.
HOSANNA: You imagined it all. You're always imagining things like that.
GUARDIAN: One on top of the other. Right out in the open.
HOSANNA: You said, on the mouth.
GUARDIAN: Yes. On the mouth.
HOSANNA: Are you sure it wasn't a little lower? Just a little further down?
GUARDIAN: No.
HOSANNA: Under the chin, perhaps?
GUARDIAN: No. They were copulating on the mouth.
HOSANNA: That's hard to believe.
GUARDIAN: Yes. *(Slight pause.)*
HOSANNA: Why were you looking?
GUARDIAN: At what?
HOSANNA: At that.
GUARDIAN: I was just looking.
HOSANNA: That's shameful, Guardian. Two flies on someone's mouth.
GUARDIAN: It wasn't anyone.
HOSANNA: Two lusty flies.
GUARDIAN: I said it wasn't anyone.
HOSANNA: What?
GUARDIAN: At least, no one important.
HOSANNA: You have to clean things off before you look at them, Guardian.
GUARDIAN: He wasn't anybody. He was dead.
HOSANNA: Dead?
GUARDIAN: Good and dead. First I looked at the flies. They were really moving back and forth. Then I looked at his lips. And then, the rest.
HOSANNA: The rest?... Was there something else?
GUARDIAN: Eyes, nose, and all that.
HOSANNA: Like a face?
GUARDIAN: Not like a face. He was dead.

HOSANNA: Really? *(She laughs.)*
GUARDIAN: Without legs.
HOSANNA: Didn't he have any legs? That doesn't make sense. All right. I think you'd better start from the beginning, Guardian. First things first. You felt slightly uneasy, you opened your eyes, and you heard the fluttering of wings. Isn't that right?
GUARDIAN: I didn't say that he didn't have any legs; I just said you couldn't see them.
HOSANNA: After the fluttering of wings, you heard the panting of the flies.
GUARDIAN: You couldn't see them because something was covering them up.
HOSANNA: Are you sure I didn't see all that too?
GUARDIAN *(Relentlessly)*: I don't know. Actually there was another pair of pants and shoes—someone else's—covering up the first pair of pants and shoes that you couldn't see, but that I imagine were there.
HOSANNA: Another pair?
GUARDIAN: I meant some other legs.
HOSANNA: That's impossible.
GUARDIAN: Not just a pair of legs all by themselves; there was another body there too.
HOSANNA: Someone else, then.
GUARDIAN: It wasn't anyone. He was dead.
HOSANNA: On top of the other one.
GUARDIAN: Or the other one on top of him. I really couldn't tell.
HOSANNA: He was either on top or underneath!
GUARDIAN: I don't know.

The crazy girl enters, carrying more metal. Guardian and Hosanna stop talking for a minute the way an aristocrat might when a servant enters the room. The crazy girl leaves.

HOSANNA: Did you say a nose or a shoe?
GUARDIAN: I said legs.
HOSANNA: And then you heard the buzzing.
GUARDIAN: That was earlier.
HOSANNA: And...?
GUARDIAN: He was dead too. Covering up part of the other one. At first that was all I saw.
HOSANNA: Oh, there were two... And then you saw someone else,

THE EVE OF THE EXECUTION

somebody who was talking.
GUARDIAN: Nobody was talking. I looked again and then I realized what it was.
HOSANNA: Guardian, are you sure you saw those flies?
GUARDIAN: There were a lot of them.
HOSANNA: A lot of flies?...
GUARDIAN: A lot of bodies. They were lying all over the place.
HOSANNA: In different places.
GUARDIAN: Piled up on each other. There must have been hundreds of them. They weren't in rows; they were lying one on top of the other.
HOSANNA: Did you see an eye? Maybe just one?
GUARDIAN: I didn't see even one eye, Hosanna. Just hundreds of them piled on top of each other.
HOSANNA: Hundreds of eyes?
GUARDIAN: No. Bodies.
HOSANNA: Any expression on their faces?
GUARDIAN: They were grinning.
HOSANNA: What was it then?
GUARDIAN: All the dry land and the fertile land was covered with dead bodies.
HOSANNA: You dreamed it all, the way some people dream about love.
GUARDIAN: I walked at least six miles in three hours. Walking two miles in an hour on top of those soft, rubbery bodies.
HOSANNA: Were they naked?
GUARDIAN: Yes, but once in a while I would step on a hat or a bone.
HOSANNA: That's ridiculous. Nobody uses hats or bones.
GUARDIAN *(Thinks for a moment):* Once I stepped on an orthopedic brace.
HOSANNA: In case you'd like to know, Guardian, that's not funny.
GUARDIAN: You know something, Hosanna? After I'd walked over miles and miles of bodies I got used to it. Yes, I started to regulate my steps and my breathing. My feet began to be able to find the most solid part of the bodies. I only looked down once.
HOSANNA: When you tripped.
GUARDIAN: No. When I stepped on a face and broke somebody's glasses.
HOSANNA: We ought to...

GUARDIAN: I was afraid. I thought I had stepped on a cockroach—that's what it sounded like—but I felt better when I saw that it was only a blind face and a pair of broken glasses.

HOSANNA: We ought to go away.

GUARDIAN: Where?

HOSANNA: To Paradise, of course.

GUARDIAN: Oh, yes… *(The crazy girl enters again, carrying more metal that she throws onto the high pile, rear. Guardian and Hosanna wait quietly, watching her. The crazy girl leaves.)* I just thought of something, Hosanna.

HOSANNA: What, Guardian?

GUARDIAN: All those people died at the same time.

HOSANNA: When do you think that was?

GUARDIAN: I don't know, but it was all at once. At the very same minute.

HOSANNA *(Astonished):* All of them? You mean all those bodies…

GUARDIAN: All at the same time.

HOSANNA: I can't believe it.

GUARDIAN: Mountains of twisted bodies that stretch out to the sea.

HOSANNA: You mean that we…?

GUARDIAN: The only ones.

HOSANNA: But somewhere, there must be…

GUARDIAN: Who knows?

HOSANNA: But someone must be alive.

GUARDIAN: I doubt it.

The crazy girl has entered again, carrying more metal. Guardian and Hosanna don't stop talking now, or even lower their voices.

HOSANNA *(Pointing to the girl):* That lousy little bitch.

GUARDIAN: I found her singing by the seashore.

HOSANNA: So there was a seashore.

GUARDIAN: She was laughing and singing.

HOSANNA: Now she has lice.

GUARDIAN: I told her to help me find you, and we shouted together all night long. *(The girl leaves.)*

HOSANNA: I know you were together, you and that lousy thing, but I'm sure you weren't looking for me.

GUARDIAN: What's her name?

HOSANNA: I suppose it's Louse.

GUARDIAN: Oh.

THE EVE OF THE EXECUTION

HOSANNA: I was the one who called out to you.
GUARDIAN: It's all the same.
HOSANNA: No, it's not the same.
GUARDIAN: No. *(A brief silence.)* You should know what happened.
HOSANNA: Before it all happened I smelled something familiar like rosemary or marmalade, something from my childhood. Then, all at once, my stomach jerked violently and it happened almost immediately afterward. There was no noise and no light, but it happened.
GUARDIAN: You must have heard the noise.
HOSANNA: No.
GUARDIAN: You're lying, Hosanna, but go on.
HOSANNA: I was in a pit. I think it was something like a grave. I had just finished eating a cracker, and I turned toward him to tell him something about…
GUARDIAN *(Interrupting)*: Toward whom?
HOSANNA: A very intelligent Greek professor who hated lobster. The place was full of people. You know, all jammed together. They were all very intelligent. Nearly everyone, except the Greek professor, was eating lobster. I had turned to him to tell him something about my family tree. Immediately afterward, without any interruption, I found myself in the grave, staring at it all.
GUARDIAN: I thought you said you didn't see anything.
HOSANNA: Not exactly. First there was the party with the laughter, the intelligent remarks and the taste of the cracker in my mouth. But afterward I was there, looking.
GUARDIAN: Looking at what?
HOSANNA: A little sand—less than a thousand grains. It began to slip through the crack, and it covered up the little insect—a kind of shell—completely. It didn't try to get away—it didn't even move—until it was entirely covered by the thousand grains of sand. While I was looking at that I completely forgot about you. Strange, isn't it?
GUARDIAN: It was an empty shell.
HOSANNA: First it was filled with sand, and then it disappeared. I didn't take my eyes away from it, and I just waited.
GUARDIAN: You might have called me.
HOSANNA: I don't remember. The smell of the bodies drifted into the grave, or whatever it was, like whiffs of smoke. I thought it was the smell of the countryside. The contact with nature. *(She laughs for*

a brief instant.) I could only move my eyes. I was stiff.
GUARDIAN: What time was it, exactly?
HOSANNA: I don't know. But the sky never changed color.
GUARDIAN: Was it a color?
HOSANNA: Yes, black.
GUARDIAN: What about the light? There was a bright glow!
HOSANNA: There wasn't anything. It was all completely black. Then Louse came along, singing, and looked into the hole.
GUARDIAN: Let's get going.
HOSANNA: I know that if I fall asleep, you'll go on without me.
GUARDIAN: We should get to Paradise tonight.
HOSANNA: All I would have to do would be to fall asleep, and you'd leave me stretched out in the cart and go off by yourself.
GUARDIAN: I've thought about it.
HOSANNA: I haven't slept for two years.
GUARDIAN: Two years?
HOSANNA: Since it happened.
GUARDIAN: Or maybe two hours.
HOSANNA: Or two years, or twenty years...
GUARDIAN: I don't remember.
HOSANNA: I can't get my mind off it. Ever since you took me out of the hole I haven't stopped looking at you. I'd never looked at you before.
GUARDIAN *(Goes to push the cart):* Are you ready?
HOSANNA: Don't move! It's time for you to be cleaned, and time for my meal. *(She shouts.)* Louse!
GUARDIAN: Nobody's going to touch me.
HOSANNA: It's time for your cleaning, no matter where we are... Louse! *(Louse appears, dragging still another nondescript piece of metal. She puts it on top of the large pile and stands perfectly still. Then, with an impassive expression on her face, she does what she's told.)* Clean his fingernails and his mustache. You don't have to take off his clothes.
She does what she's told. Guardian lets her.
GUARDIAN: Sometimes I don't think anything has happened, Hosanna.
HOSANNA: A massage, or just talcum?
GUARDIAN: Massage. There are times when I even start thinking that it's beautiful. That the countryside has always been like this, covered with naked bodies.

THE EVE OF THE EXECUTION

HOSANNA: A dead mother-nature, right?

GUARDIAN: Sometimes...

HOSANNA *(Interrupting):* Ointment?

GUARDIAN: No.

HOSANNA: Gargle. Just once to get the bad taste out of your mouth.

GUARDIAN: Sometimes I think you stop looking at me, just for a minute.

HOSANNA: A little saliva on his eyebrows too.

GUARDIAN: Sometimes I don't think we've changed.

HOSANNA: Wash his eyes!

GUARDIAN: Sometimes I think you love me.

HOSANNA: I just watch out for you, dear. That's all.

GUARDIAN: Sometimes I want...

HOSANNA *(With a tone full of resentment):* Yes, you want to hit me with your fist on Sundays and other holy days.

GUARDIAN: Sometimes...

HOSANNA: Now sprinkle holy water on him. *(Louse takes a bottle out of the cart and sprinkles it on Guardian.)* All right. *(Louse leaves quietly.)* I want to eat.

GUARDIAN *(Going up to the cart and pulling objects out of it):* Do you want me to fix the bed for you?

HOSANNA: No. I want to eat.

GUARDIAN: An aperitif to begin with?

HOSANNA: No.

GUARDIAN: Celery and salads are good for you, Hosanna.

HOSANNA: They give me gas.

GUARDIAN: Today I have a surprise for you... *(Raising his voice, as though calling far off to Louse.)* Louse, serve the soup!

HOSANNA *(Brightening up):* Soup?

GUARDIAN: Well... almost. Actually, it could be anything at all.

HOSANNA: I know what it is. It's terrible.

GUARDIAN: With sauce or without?

HOSANNA: On what?

GUARDIAN: The same thing as yesterday.

HOSANNA: Without, thanks.

GUARDIAN *(Shouting at Louse, offstage):* Without sauce...! I think there are still a few crumbs left from the wedding cake.

HOSANNA: I don't want them.

GUARDIAN: Anything else, or are you satisfied?

HOSANNA: Completely unsatisfied.
GUARDIAN: Louse, clear away the dishes, we're going out to the main hall. *(Louse enters with another piece of metal. Guardian pushes the cart to the other side of the stage.)* Now let's trade. It's almost like a honeymoon.
HOSANNA: Don't put me so I'm facing the sun: I have to look at you.
GUARDIAN: We haven't seen the sun since it happened. Don't be unfair. You know perfectly well that I want to kill you, but I would never do it without your consent.
HOSANNA: You'll have to wait.
GUARDIAN: Will it be long?
HOSANNA: No, not long.

Louse leaves. A brief pause. Guardian takes up a story that has apparently been interrupted.

GUARDIAN: I'll tell you some more about my life. We were at four and a half years old, weren't we?
HOSANNA *(Indifferently)*: Yes.
GUARDIAN: All right, two months later I got up on a chair and looked out a window for the first time.
HOSANNA: What was it like?
GUARDIAN: Don't interrupt. I looked outside. Then I realized that I wasn't looking out, but in.
HOSANNA: What?
GUARDIAN: Yes. Yes, it was the inside of another room. The window faced another locked room.
HOSANNA: Then it wasn't a window.
GUARDIAN: Yes, it was. It just didn't look out. It faced a kind of closet.
HOSANNA: What's so strange about that?
GUARDIAN: Three days later, that is, when I was four months and twenty seven days old…
HOSANNA: Can't you go a little faster?
GUARDIAN: I have to tell you my whole life, minute by minute. I remember that two hours after I got up on the chair…
HOSANNA *(Distracted)*: Do we have a long way to go before we get to Paradise? We ought to be going right away.
GUARDIAN: Two hours after I got up on the chair, when my age was exactly…
HOSANNA: Is it really very far?
GUARDIAN: I don't think so.

THE EVE OF THE EXECUTION

Louse enters with another piece of metal. The girl stands completely still for a moment, as though absorbed in something that no one else can see or hear. She emits a sort of soft cry that seems almost melodic. Her face lights up with a smile for the first time. Then she doubles over, her arms crossed and holding her stomach. She falls to her knees, emitting guttural cries. Nearly doubled up into a ball, she crawls off on all fours like an animal.

HOSANNA: What's she saying?

GUARDIAN: She says that she's pregnant.

HOSANNA: What?

GUARDIAN: Pregnant.

HOSANNA: But, of course, she isn't.

GUARDIAN: I don't know.

HOSANNA: She's always spouting nonsense. She's an idiot.

GUARDIAN: She's getting bigger.

HOSANNA: That shapeless hulk of old rags.

GUARDIAN: She's getting fatter every day.

HOSANNA: Do you mean to tell me that she's really pregnant?

GUARDIAN: That's what she says, that's what she sings, and she's getting fat. That's all I know.

HOSANNA *(Shouting)*: You mean that you can accept the fact and be so indifferent about it?

GUARDIAN: What fact?

HOSANNA: You mean that you're proud of getting her pregnant?

GUARDIAN *(Shouting)*: I don't mean anything!

HOSANNA: But that's obviously what you're saying.

GUARDIAN: Maybe.

HOSANNA *(Shouting)*: You filthy old man! You rape her over my body while I'm asleep. You get her pregnant under my own clothes. You did it right here, in this very cart!

GUARDIAN *(Shouting)*: Shut up! It wasn't me...

HOSANNA *(Hysterical)*: And who else could it have been...? You know that all the rest of them are dead. There isn't a living thing left. We're all alone.

GUARDIAN: We have been for two hours.

HOSANNA: For two years... We've always been alone. You filthy beast!

GUARDIAN *(Shouting)*: Shut up! You know I'm impotent!

HOSANNA: Yes, I know. I know. Our frustrating wedding night lasted thirty years.

GUARDIAN: I haven't even touched her. I can't stand her. She's like a swollen animal.
HOSANNA: You fixed things up somehow. You were asking for a massage a while ago.
GUARDIAN: We're going to have to get to Paradise today.
HOSANNA: What for? I don't want to move. We're already in Paradise, and you never even told me. You're an impotent Adam and I'm a paralytic virgin Eve, and a demented, pregnant, avenging angel is prodding us on. *(Louse comes in without any metal.)*
GUARDIAN *(Looking at her)*: It must have been me, and I just don't remember. That would be wonderful, Hosanna, wouldn't it?
A brief pause. At this point the light begins to grow dim.
HOSANNA: Don't you see?
GUARDIAN: What?
HOSANNA: We have to repopulate the world. *(She laughs.)*
GUARDIAN: We can begin by inventing sin.
HOSANNA: It's scandalous! What will they say about us?
GUARDIAN: Who?
HOSANNA: That's right. We're alone in Paradise. *(A brief pause.)* And yet, it all depends on us.
GUARDIAN: What depends on us?
HOSANNA: Making it all over again, reconstructing the world, inventing life… Look, that almost sounds convincing: life! *(Guardian seems distracted.)* Did you hear me? *(Guardian makes a grimace.)*
GUARDIAN: Something's wrong with me. I feel nauseated.
HOSANNA: Every time I talk to you about life the same thing happens. Don't get the metal all dirty! *(Guardian leaves. Louse is sitting on the ground, leaning back against the metal, her arms crossed over her stomach. She doesn't move. Hosanna, on the other side of the stage, standing stock still, stares at her. She slowly goes over to her. When she is next to her, she looks at her for a moment. She tries to prod her with her foot. Finally she speaks to her. A soft light is on Hosanna. Louse seems almost like a silhouette. Everything else is in soft shadows.)* Did you hear me, Louse? *(Silence.)* I know you can hear me… *(Silence.)* After it all happened, you appeared. Both of you came up, above the grave, outlined against the black sky. Why…? Why…? You didn't want to see me, but you had to scream. You were with him. I thought he might have disappeared like a star, but no, he came along with you.

THE EVE OF THE EXECUTION

(*Silence.*) Who are you, anyway?... A kind of animal. Instinct incarnate. But a woman like me has an entire life behind her, a tradition, an obligation... I know how to control myself, I know how to act. I can control my emotional outbursts, well, not outbursts, but... I have principles, a set of values, duties. I haven't taken life lightly; it's always been a very serious matter to me. (*A brief silence.*) You filthy beggar—you got pregnant in the mud: that's what you deserved! And the worst is yet to come. You haven't swallowed a little pea. It's something living that grows like a blind fish. (*Suddenly going to pieces.*) I... I would have liked to have a son... I wish that creature of yours were gnawing at my stomach... I even envy the air around you. Your very existence is a thorn in my side. I wish I could die... I'm a tiny bit of ashes, waiting terrified to be scattered by a puff of wind. (*A painful silence. Then a brusque change.*) You're a nobody. A nothing... I have a cart and a husband to push it. I have a wedding gown. If Guardian and I don't fit in the cart together, that's no business of yours. But we won't sleep just anywhere: not in the mud, and not on all those corpses. You're shapeless, ugly, a vegetable. (*An oppressive silence.*) And, besides, Guardian is... incrusted in my life like a louse under the skin. If he would only listen to me when I tell him something foolish like "I'm afraid," or "Let's find a little shade,"... but that's asking a great deal. If I could only put my hand on his knee and hope... but perhaps that's too much as well. If only I could look at him and he would look back at me... but maybe that too... if only... once... I could... (*Hosanna stands still for a moment, immersed in a desolate silence. Then, brusquely, she spits directly into Louse's face, and shouts at her*): You whore! (*Hosanna limps quickly to the other side of the stage, and goes into the shadows. She does not come out again. Guardian enters, somewhat hesitantly and slightly disturbed. He looks around for Hosanna.*)

GUARDIAN: Hosanna! (*Hosanna, in the shadows, does not move. Guardian, disconcerted, stands still for a moment. Then, very slowly, he goes up to Louse, almost as though hypnotized by her silent presence. When he is very near he talks to her, as though uttering a private monologue out loud.*) So, then, I raped you... If I did, I don't remember it. But I might as well accept the fact. What I could never do took place without me, I wasn't even involved... And it happened with you, a poor, aimless mad woman. How long has it been since you got pregnant? When did all this happen? When did we become the only survivors? If I could only find that out, I would know if I really ravished you in a deep, forgotten dream, or if it all happened before, when the others were living, and I was dying day by day. Oh, revelation of the world! It all depends on you, my visionary whore, on your shameful, incoherent memories, on your chant, on your incomprehensible burden... When I first saw you, you were a black dot on the edge of the disaster. I thought you were a bird or an animal, digging around in the rotting flesh... but you were singing. Why did you start to scream when you saw Hosanna sinking into the hole that was opening in the ground?... She was going down, she was disappearing at last, and you got her out... What did you want? What do you want?... What did I do? What made you give her back to me? *(A heavy silence.)* She... she hates me. She doesn't know everything. She doesn't know that I have a good imagination. Sometimes—not very often—I can even remember my earlier life, and she doesn't know it. *(A brief pause.)* A long time ago I had another wife. The only thing I remember about her is that she had tiny feet and a blue vein running across her neck. I think, but I'm not really sure about it, that we had a baby who was born dead. Hosanna must suspect, because sometimes she laughs to herself. *(Silence. Guardian doesn't look at Louse now. He turns his back to her and speaks directly to the audience.)* What was I saying?... Something about time or the long road to Paradise where a man can feel safe. They say that old people aren't killed there. I don't believe it, but that's what I tell her so she won't have to suffer. How could there be a place—even if it is Paradise—where they don't throw old people into a pit full of sawdust, the way they do everywhere else; where they don't round them up, order them to have babies, castrate or exterminate them? I don't believe in it, but it's nice to think of, to pretend you believe. It could be that... no one knows... there might be... a day... *(Silence.)*

HOSANNA *(From the shadows)*: What if we hang her?
GUARDIAN *(Startled)*: Were you there all the time?
HOSANNA: Yes.
GUARDIAN: Spying. *(The light comes up very slowly.)*
HOSANNA: What if we hang her?
GUARDIAN: A person might think it was getting to be morning if we didn't know that's impossible.
HOSANNA: What if we hang her?
GUARDIAN *(Distracted)*: Huh?

THE EVE OF THE EXECUTION

HOSANNA: Smother her.
GUARDIAN: Louse?
HOSANNA: Yes.
GUARDIAN: What for...?
HOSANNA: To be doing something. To finish it.
GUARDIAN: In order to finish, we have to get to Paradise.
HOSANNA: I'll get into the cart, and you can tell me when we're there. *(Silence.)*
GUARDIAN: What if we abandon her?
HOSANNA: And go on alone?
GUARDIAN: Yes.
HOSANNA: She'll die.
GUARDIAN: I doubt it.
HOSANNA: She's going to have a baby. She'll die if she's left alone.
GUARDIAN: I don't think she cares.
HOSANNA: What if we kill her first?
GUARDIAN: She'll die then too.
HOSANNA: Oh. I hadn't thought about that. *(Silence.)*
GUARDIAN: Are we bad, Hosanna?
HOSANNA: No, Guardian. We're pure.
GUARDIAN: There aren't any pure ones left.
HOSANNA: Not even one.
GUARDIAN: Only pregnant Louse is left. *(A brief silence.)*
HOSANNA: I have an idea.
GUARDIAN: Keep it to yourself.
HOSANNA: Let's crucify her.
GUARDIAN: That's pretty common. Everyone does it.
HOSANNA: Let's bury her.
GUARDIAN: That's hard to do.
HOSANNA: Let's beat her.
GUARDIAN: I don't have the strength. I would die.
HOSANNA: Let's cover her up with the metal until she disappears from sight.
GUARDIAN: I'd never do that.
HOSANNA: Why not?
GUARDIAN: We'd be wasting the metal. It's the only thing we have left.
HOSANNA: It would be worth it.
GUARDIAN: I don't know.

HOSANNA: Don't be so stingy.
GUARDIAN: It's *my* metal.
HOSANNA: Do it for her.
GUARDIAN: I'm always having to lose something.
HOSANNA: It's a small sacrifice. This way no one can put the blame on us.
GUARDIAN: Maybe you're right. It's the only way not to have any regrets. *(Guardian goes to the rear and looks for a moment at Louse who hasn't moved and who doesn't seem to see him. Louse is curled up, withdrawn. Guardian drags Louse behind a pile of metal. He suddenly throws her to the ground. Louse is hidden from view. Guardian emerges, standing up. Guardian takes a piece of metal from the top of the pile, holds it in the air for a moment, and then lets it drop on Louse. Each piece that he drops on her body is accompanied by a type of litany that Hosanna recites in a dull, monotonous tone.)* "Guide her steps that she will not stumble."
HOSANNA: Keep her from evil, Lord.
Another piece of metal is thrown on Louse.
GUARDIAN: "Give her strength in her hour of trial..."
HOSANNA: Keep her from evil, Lord.
More metal is thrown on her body.
GUARDIAN: "Let her not be unprepared for the trumpets of Judgment Day."
HOSANNA: Keep her from evil, Lord.
More metal is thrown on her body.
GUARDIAN: "At the holy hour of Martyrdom..."
HOSANNA: Keep her from evil, Lord.
More metal on her body.
GUARDIAN: "May the burden of her life be as naught..."
HOSANNA: Keep her from evil, Lord.
More metal on her body.
GUARDIAN: "May love inspire our actions..."
HOSANNA: Keep her from evil, Lord.
More metal on her body.
GUARDIAN: "Forgive her weaknesses, Lord, and comfort her in the hour of her death."
HOSANNA: The holy water. *(Hosanna sprinkles the metal with holy water from the bottle. Louse has not opened her mouth to groan even once. She is completely engulfed by the metal. For a moment Hosanna and Guardian stand next to each other, not moving. Suddenly, from beneath the pile of metal comes a*

THE EVE OF THE EXECUTION

blood-curdling scream followed by moans.) The pains are starting.
GUARDIAN: Already?
HOSANNA: Yes. She's going into labor.
GUARDIAN: Is it bad?
HOSANNA: It's natural.
GUARDIAN: Like death?
HOSANNA: Yes, as natural as death.
GUARDIAN: Like us?
HOSANNA: Yes, as natural as we are.
GUARDIAN: Then she's all right.
More cries, softer but more urgent.
HOSANNA: They're coming closer together now.
GUARDIAN: Do you think that... that thing will be born.
HOSANNA: What?
GUARDIAN: What has to be born.
HOSANNA: I don't know.
GUARDIAN: It would be terrible: a punishment.
HOSANNA: She thinks we're going to help her.
GUARDIAN: Yes, she does.
HOSANNA: And no one will be there.
GUARDIAN: Let's go.
HOSANNA: She'll be all alone.
GUARDIAN: Alone.
HOSANNA: We're only bystanders.
GUARDIAN: We've lost the only thing we had: the metal. *(Long, stifled moans.)*
HOSANNA: She's starting to give birth. She's calling us.
GUARDIAN: I can't hear a thing. I'm too excited.
HOSANNA: You should have piled it on top of me.
GUARDIAN: It's too late now. *They listen for a moment.*
HOSANNA: She's not calling us now.
GUARDIAN: What's she doing?
HOSANNA: She's trying to breathe.
They listen again.
GUARDIAN: Do you think anything has been born?
HOSANNA: What difference does it make? If something was born, it must be metal.
A long silence. Then the loud cry of a woman giving birth is heard. The crying and panting persist until they culminate in a final, piercing scream. Guardian and

Hosanna have remained completely still. Silence.
GUARDIAN: What now?
HOSANNA: Now, nothing.
GUARDIAN: Then...
HOSANNA: It's finished.
GUARDIAN: But maybe...
HOSANNA: It's finished.
GUARDIAN: Everything?
HOSANNA: Everything. *(Hosanna moves to one of the sides of the stage.)* Come on. Paradise is waiting for us.
Guardian goes over to the cart and begins to push it.
GUARDIAN: Let's go.
Hosanna exits, limping. Guardian is going to follow her, pushing the cart, when he realizes that he has left the bottle of holy water on the ground, next to the metal. He goes back, picks it up and looks at it for a moment. Then, brusquely, he breaks the bottle against the metal while keeping hold of its neck.
HOSANNA'S VOICE *(From offstage)*: What are you doing, Guardian?
GUARDIAN: Nothing. We forgot the holy water. *(Holding the broken bottle in one hand and pushing the cart with the other, he goes out. The light begins to grow dim. A strange glow emanates from behind the metal. From offstage a thump is heard, and a muffled cry. Guardian enters immediately afterward. He is pushing the cart in which we see the bridal crown and the torn veil, stained with blood. He is still gripping the broken bottle. He looks back. Then he shudders and says:)* And the evening and the morning were the first day of the world. *(He talks into the empty cart.)* Let us repopulate the world, my dear heart... *(Offering the broken, bloody bottle.)* You're hungry, but don't start screaming—we have to hide from the avenging angel... Lord, we have killed in Thy name, according to Thy will! Amen. *(Guardian goes slowly off, pushing the cart. The light dims and softly turns to darkness.)*

THE END

A DOZEN ORGIES

Other books by Robert S. Rudder:

Magic Realism in Cervantes (Translation of work by Arturo Serrano Plaja): Univ. of California Pr.

The Life of Lazarillo de Tormes (Edition and translation): Frederick Ungar Publishing Co.

The Orgy (Edition and translation of Latin American drama): Univ. of California Pr.

The Literature of Spain in English Translation: a Bibliography: Frederick Ungar Publishing Co.

City of Kings (Translation of work by Rosario Castellanos): Latin American Literary Review Pr.

Nazarin (Translation of work by Benito Pérez Galdós): Latin American Literary Review Pr.

The Medicine Man (Translation of work by Francisco Rojas González): Latin American Literary Review Pr.

Solitaire of Love (Translation of work by Cristina Peri Rossi): Duke University Pr.

The Forbidden (Translation of work by Benito Pérez Galdós): Cambridge Scholars Pub.

The Paradox of Santa Teresa de Jesús: A Study in Will and Humility: Edwin Mellen Pr.

Intimate Disasters (Translation of work by Cristina Peri Rossi): Latin American Literary Review Pr.: (Forthcoming).

ROBERT S. RUDDER

Ebooks by Robert S. Rudder:

The Life of Lazarillo de Tormes (Edition and translation).

Tales of the White Knight: Tirant lo Blanc (Edition and translation of work by Joanot Martorell).

La Celestina (Edition in Spanish, with glossary and notes).

Afternoon of the Dinosaur (Translation of work by Cristina Peri Rossi).

The Celestina (Annotated English translation of work by Fernando de Rojas).

A Dozen Orgies: Latin American Plays of the Twentieth Century (Anthology of one-act dramas in English translation).

Made in the USA
Middletown, DE
02 July 2018